Implementing the Montessori Method

Learner-Centered Education From Birth Through Adolescence

Trisha Thompson-Willingham and Susan Zoll

Foreword by Erica Moretti

Teachers College Press
Teachers College, Columbia University

Published by Teachers College Press,® 1234 Amsterdam Avenue, New York, NY 10027

Photo of plant by Eglantine Shala / Pixabay. WIndow by Laura Ohlman / Unsplash.

Library of Congress Cataloging-in-Publication Data

Names: Thompson-Willingham, Trisha author | Zoll, Susan author
Title: Implementing the Montessori method : learner-centered education from birth through adolescence / Trisha Thompson-Willingham and Susan Zoll ; foreword by Erica Moretti.
Description: New York, NY : Teachers College Press, [2026] | Includes bibliographical references and index. | Summary: "This comprehensive overview includes vignettes for each classroom level demonstrating the Montessori pedagogy in action, as well as alignment to research confirming the effectiveness of this instructional approach"—Provided by publisher.
Identifiers: LCCN 2025041822 (print) | LCCN 2025041823 (ebook) | ISBN 9780807784112 paperback | ISBN 9780807783665 hardcover | ISBN 9780807784129 ebook
Subjects: LCSH: Montessori method of education
Classification: LCC LB1029.M75 T46 2026 (print) | LCC LB1029.M75 (ebook)
LC record available at https://lccn.loc.gov/2025041822
LC ebook record available at https://lccn.loc.gov/2025041823

ISBN 978-0-8077-8411-2 (paper)
ISBN 978-0-8077-8366-5 (hardcover)
ISBN 978-0-8077-8412-9 (ebook)

Printed on acid-free paper
Manufactured in the United States of America

Praise for *Implementing the Montessori Method*

"You're holding a treasure. This authoritative guide reveals what education can be—painting a vivid picture of the Montessori Method in practice from birth through adolescence. Developmentally wise, holistic, and rooted in science, the Montessori Method is as relevant today as it was a century ago. Here, two of its most knowledgeable practitioners illuminate exactly how this transformative approach informs all aspects of educational practice, from curriculum design to the physical setup of the classroom and school culture."

—**Angela Duckworth**, co-director, Behavior Change for Good Initiative, The Wharton School, University of Pennsylvania

"Backed by research and decades of educational insight, this book demonstrates how Montessori education empowers students to thrive at every stage of human development—academically, socially, and emotionally. It is a clear and compelling resource for educators, parents, and anyone passionate about learner-centered teaching."

—**Munir Shivji**, executive director, American Montessori Society

"This incredible book is not for Montessori educators only, but a must-read for all educators. It takes phrases that have become stock sayings, almost clichés in education—like 'preparation for life,' 'individualized learning,' 'student-centered,' 'agency,' or 'character development'—and shows us what these concepts can actually look like when well implemented in classrooms. If you've ever wondered why Montessori-educated children become such awesome adults, this book is for you! Highly recommended."

—**Ellen Galinsky**, president of Families and Work Institute, author of *Mind in the Making* and *The Breakthrough Years*

"I highly recommend this book for anyone seeking to understand how Montessori education supports children's growth and full development from birth through adolescence. Through vivid classroom stories, research insights, and reflections from Montessori alumni, it beautifully illustrates how Montessori environments cultivate curiosity, independence, and compassion. Grounded in both evidence and lived experience, it affirms that Montessori is not just an educational method but a lifelong approach to human development and potential."

—**Judith Cunningham**, chief strategic officer, Montessori Model UN, NGO in Special Consultative Status with ECOSOC

"This book is a great read for parents and teachers new to Montessori education. It highlights Maria Montessori's logical, comprehensive, and well-considered approach toward education that supports knowledge and skills, but at the same time helps children build strong characters and personalities. It is the sum of all parts, the sum of all different components that make Montessori such a strong educational method."

—**Chris Willemsen**, business unit manager, Nienhuis Montessori, the Netherlands

"*Implementing the Montessori Method* is comprehensive and detailed, and yet a joy to read. Thompson-Willingham and Zoll will take you by the hand and walk you gently through the full journey of a Montessori child, pointing with awe and wonder at the sights along the way. This book is a must-read for anyone who's ever encountered a Montessori school and wondered, 'What are they doing in there? And why?'"

—**Corey Borgman**, director of education and outreach, Montessori Science Program, University of Virginia

"This book beautifully connects the timeless foundations of Montessori education with the realities of today's classrooms. It shows how Maria Montessori's intentional, learner-centered approach continues to shape modern teaching. It offers a clear, compelling synthesis of history, theory, and practice that feels both deeply grounded and refreshingly relevant."

—**Amy Schmidtke**, director of educational practice, Buffett Early Childhood Institute at the University of Nebraska, and editor of *The Intentional Teacher*

"The authors reinspire the essence of Montessori education with profound depth and enduring relevance in our theory. Through their thoughtful integration of contemporary research and Montessori principles, they reaffirm that when evidence and philosophy converge, our practice is both renewed and strengthened for today's diverse educational landscape."

—**Carrie Horwitz Lang**, director of Montessori, clinical assistant professor, Loyola University Maryland, School of Education

"This book is a rich and timely reminder of the power of Montessori education across every stage of life. Thompson-Willingham and Zoll beautifully highlight the lifelong impact of the approach through alumni reflections, the often-overlooked planes of development (adolescence and beyond), and the essential role of the trained Montessori guide. This book showcases why Montessori belongs at the heart of all teacher preparation programs."

—**Jihane Mrad**, director of thought leadership, *Trust for Learning*

This book is dedicated to Dan, who always perceives my practical knowledge as amazing intellect. I am forever grateful to Esprit, Sarah, and Harper for teaching me so much more about child development than I could have ever imagined. I have deep gratitude for my family and friends in this Montessori life.

—Trisha

So very grateful for this Montessori journey and treasure the privilege of learning alongside such generous guides. Unending love and gratitude to my family. Your patience provided space for experiences to be transformed into words on a page.

—Susan

Contents

Foreword

Maria Montessori remains one of the most influential—and most misunderstood—educators of the 20th century. Many people recognize her name because of the schools that claim her legacy, but few know much about her life or the educational approach she developed. Those unfamiliar with Montessori education often picture children choosing their own activities or working with wooden materials, but they rarely grasp what actually happens in these classrooms. Even people with some exposure to Montessori tend to rely on scattered impressions or anecdotes. These glimpses, though based in reality, often miss the structured and research-driven foundation behind her work. Without deeper engagement, it's easy to overlook how deliberately she built her method to support children's development in thoughtful and systematic ways.

Although Montessori schools continue to thrive across the United States and attract growing numbers of families, many people still misinterpret the essence of her educational philosophy. Too often, public understanding reduces the Montessori method to a set of consumer goods: a bed, a shelf, or a toy kit marketed as part of a minimalist parenting lifestyle. But Montessori never intended her approach to be fragmented or commercialized. Likewise, though she is often grouped with more esoteric approaches such as Waldorf education and criticized for lacking scientific rigor, Montessori was, in fact, a scientist at heart. Her method emerged from scientific observation and a profound respect for the child's autonomy, development, and dignity. Her method was built on systematic observation, experimentation, and a deep commitment to evidence-based practice—an approach that set her apart from both mystical educational philosophies and more conventional progressive models developed by educators like John Dewey.

Implementing the Montessori Method: Learner-Centered Education from Birth Through Adolescence brings readers back to the heart of Montessori's vision. In today's landscape of "Montessori-inspired" trends, Thompson-Willingham and Zoll call attention to the depth and coherence of Montessori's pedagogy. They make it clear that a central feature of Montessori education—the prepared environment—involves more than curating a space with select materials. It must reflect a unified educational philosophy centered on purposeful engagement, independence, and the unfolding of each child's potential.

This book offers a clear and thoughtful overview of Maria Montessori's approach to education, following her educational method from birth through age 18. Thompson-Willingham and Zoll explain the key principles of the Montessori method—such as careful observation, developmental stages, and the role of the learning environment—while also connecting Montessori's ideas to both past and present research on child development. They draw comparisons between Montessori and her contemporaries, and link her thinking to today's scientific studies, showing how her approach still speaks to the needs of children now. Along the way, they also take on urgent issues such as racism, discrimination, and inequality, and ask how Montessori's method can respond. By doing so, they open up new ways of thinking about how this method can grow and stay relevant in today's diverse and complex world.

Most important, perhaps, this book provides us with a particularly intimate view of what this education looks like in practice, as it takes place in the Montessori classrooms where this method continues to shape the lives of students. Readers of this book are given the opportunity to feel like a Montessori teacher themselves, carefully observing the unfolding of each child's potential within a prepared environment and documenting changes in both the child and the classroom during a specific developmental phase. These glimpses into classroom life not only ground theory in lived experience but also challenge widespread misconceptions about Montessori education—particularly the oversimplified view of the prepared environment. By grounding theory in lived experience, Thompson-Willingham and Zoll provide a nuanced and practical understanding of how Montessori's ideas continue to shape—and are shaped by—evolving educational realities.

The book shows in rich detail how Montessori environments support young people as increasingly active agents in their own developmental journeys, and how Montessori education works to nurture individual agency and to cultivate a deep, ecologically grounded sense of global responsibility. Rather than offering a static or compartmentalized education, Montessori proposed a transformative pedagogy that prepares young people to understand their role in shaping a more just and sustainable world. It hardly needs mentioning that such an education is needed today more than ever.

—Erica Moretti
Associate Professor, Modern Languages and Cultures, FIT
Author, *The Best Weapon for Peace: Maria Montessori, Education, and Children's Rights*

Acknowledgments

The authors are deeply appreciative to Teachers College Press for including a third book dedicated to Montessori education in their expansive library. We are especially grateful to our editors, Emily Spangler and Sarah Jubar, who along with their team bring clarity and wisdom to this work.

We are extremely grateful to our colleague, Dr. Erica Moretti, for her gracious Foreword. As a historian and researcher, her insights are invaluable to our understanding of the political and social contexts of Dr. Montessori's work. We share in her aim to bring Montessori's writing to a new generation of educators who seek to bring a "transformative pedagogy" to all children.

We also wish to express how thankful we are to our "Montessori Constellation"—the many individuals and organizations who create a sense of belonging for children and adults alike. A simple request, and we were welcomed into schools to (re)live our own Montessori experience. Walking into classrooms, noting interactions between adults and students, and respectfully observing children engaged in their work, allowed us to remember our own path in Montessori education. Thank you to Mountaintop Montessori, a wonderful community for families, for opening their arms to this project and supporting us in all ways, including generously providing permission to include photos of your sweet children. Austin Robey, you were a saint with the photos. Susan Kennedy, Karla Gonzalez, Ailish McGaughey, Jalen Jackson, Alma Scheible, Brittney West, Lisa Wolfe, Jennifer Hoyt Tidwell, Britt Gendell, and Griffin Harvey—thank you for sharing your wonderful classrooms with us. To the Montessori School of Durham and Laura Jackman, your work with infants is so inspiring. Thank you also to J. T. Williams Montessori High School and Steven Cates—your program is really special.

And to the many Montessori alumni who generously shared stories about their experience as Montessori students: Your insights serve as confirmation of Dr. Montessori's pedagogical approach! Equal measure of gratitude to the many representatives of Montessori organizations who provided input about their work in the field—Julia Volkman, Pamela Green, Corey Borgman, Tim Seldin, faculty from Sarasota University, Judith Cunningham, Leslie Woodford, Jai Brisbon, Mirka Vickova, Katie Keller Wood, Margarita Diaz, Dr. Gulzar Babool, Judi Orion, Sara Suchman, Courtney Reim, Nancy Lindeman, Lucie Brixi Tamasova, and Joc Campbell. We welcome future researchers to build on this work and develop a more detailed census that will make visible the incredible expansion of Montessori education here in the United States and globally.

We'd also like to acknowledge Terry Millie and his generosity in sharing his insightful Hexavium (see Chapter 5). His visual representation of the elementary curriculum brings clarity to novice and expert alike regarding the rich learning experiences available in Montessori classrooms.

Special thanks are extended to members of the Relation-Centered Education Network, including Dr. Alexander "Sasha" Sidorkin, California State University; Dr. Leah O'Toole, Maynooth University in Ireland; and Dr. Iram Siraj, University of Oxford (Emeritus) and Distinguished Visiting Research Professor, Maynooth University. A note of recognition is also extended to Emer Bryden for her doctoral studies in relational listening.

More thanks to our colleagues and friends, Jean Peters, Katie Keller Wood, Randi Ellenport, and Carol Randa, for sharing precious time to offer collegial feedback on chapters of this book.

And special consideration is extended to the very foundation of the Montessori Constellation: We wish to acknowledge leadership from the American Montessori Society (AMS), Munir Shivji, Executive Director; the Association Montessori Internationale (AMI), Lynne Lawrence, Executive Director; the International Montessori Council (IMC), Executive Director Tim Seldin; and Nienhuis Montessori, with special thanks to Chris Willemsen. Finally, we're so grateful for our global Montessori community, the educators, administrators, Teacher Education Program (TEP) faculty, researchers, advocates, and families—your efforts uphold the highest quality of education for all children.

CHAPTER 1

Introduction

What if education were designed to intentionally guide each individual through the human experience so they may flourish? The curriculum, the learning environment, even the approach to delivering instruction would need to be deeply aligned to each stage of development.

What if education prepared students to recognize their own strengths while simultaneously developing their ever-expanding sense of responsibility and commitment to themselves, their community, and ultimately to the world? It would require that students nurture these skills—first through practice within the classroom, and over time extended through apprenticeship, expanding from their immediate environment to the wider community, all in preparation for their existence as a global citizen.

How would this system of education support its teachers, administrators, families? What state, national, and international organizations would be needed to uphold such a well-designed pedagogy? The education system would require teacher preparation programs, accreditation standards, curriculum and classroom materials, professional development, and advocacy organizations (among others) to maintain the highest level of quality offered in Montessori schools. This work would all be in service of meeting the cognitive, physical, and social and emotional needs of its students.

Gracious reader, if you've selected this book, there's a strong probability you're searching for a path to teaching and learning that leads with humanistic values without sacrificing rich content. You may have some understanding of Montessori education, but you'd like a clearer vision of what is offered in Montessori classrooms. This book serves as a map to journey through classrooms, highlighting their relevance at each stage of human development.

The text offers readers a view of one pedagogy—Montessori education—exploring its application in learning environments serving the youngest children up to and including classrooms supporting young adults. The authors have carefully woven threads of current research to support the pedagogical approach to teaching and learning developed by Dr. Maria Montessori more than a hundred years ago. Over this same period, conventional education has researched, renamed, redefined instruction and debated curriculum through innumerable iterations. Montessorians, however, have remained steadfast in their work in classrooms, refining a vision of education to "create a new humanity . . . inspiring children to become global citizens by utilizing their cognitive, emotional, and spiritual potential to create a better world" (Cunningham, 2017, p. 20).

We begin by offering a brief overview of Dr. Montessori and the pedagogy she developed (Chapter 2). Special attention is given to her approach to instruction aligned to children's development (sensitive periods, planes of development). The reader then visits Montessori classrooms at each age level: infant and toddler environments, also known as 0–3 classrooms (Chapter 3); early childhood, or 3–6 classrooms (Chapter 4); elementary, or 6–12 classrooms (Chapter 5); and middle and high school or adolescent, 12–18 classrooms (Chapter 6). We hope you'll see yourself as an invited guest opening a door to observe these different learning environments, exploring each classroom's materials and learning about the students and educators and their collaborative work in the classroom.

Each classroom chapter is designed as a Montessori triptych offering views of the child, the environment, and the teacher interwoven with current research related to human development and instructional practices. Together they reveal an integrated scope and sequence of learning from birth through high school. To provide an authentic vision of what happens at each age level, we've opted to take part in our own personal Montessori journey, visiting Montessori schools to conduct observations to learn directly from educators working in the field. Each age level begins with a short classroom observation, offering a snapshot of a morning work cycle for that particular age group. You'll experience a selection of classroom materials and how they support students' development, specifically, their physical, cognitive, and character development. And finally, each view of the classroom concludes with a discussion of the role of the educator. As members of Teachstone, an organization that supports classroom quality, pointed out, "(m)any measures of quality—particularly those used in K-12 settings—rarely acknowledge adjustments to teaching practice that correspond to children's development over time" (2023, p. 8). To address this concern, we've highlighted two key elements at the heart of the Montessori pedagogy: (1) the educators' deep knowledge of children's development, as well as (2) the instructional adjustments they make in response to children's development from birth through young adulthood.

We conclude our classroom visits with retrospective accounts from Montessori alumni, in response to Adele Diamond's (2015) call to those researching human development:

> I would like to encourage the field of human development to take as its charge: How can we help children (and help the adults in their lives to help the children) navigate their growing up so they grow into people we would all be proud to know—people who are upright, honest, considerate, compassionate, kind, caring, self-confident yet humble, proud but not arrogant, conscientious, bright, capable, playful, full of joy and a sense of wonder, committed to making a contribution—regardless of a child's nationality or country of birth, ethnicity, or gender, healthy or challenged, born into affluence or poverty, strife or peace? (p. 288)

Diamond made two recommendations to meet these objectives. First, researchers should conduct more studies with real-world application. Second, these studies should gather direct feedback from participants who took part in the intervention or program. Diamond proposed learning about participants' experiences through qualitative data-gathering. Could they recall key moments or experiences? Did participants see themselves differently as a result of being part of the program? These questions resonated for us, and we were curious to learn directly from those who had been enrolled as students in Montessori classrooms. Through retrospective accounts, Montessori alumni generously shared memories of being Montessori students. Some of their recollections, titled Student Reflections, are sprinkled throughout Chapters 3 through 6, highlighting key classroom experiences. Chapter 6 includes their self-analysis relating how their learning in Montessori classrooms shaped their academic pursuits and roles in the workplace.

Finally, the field of Montessori education is ever-expanding. According to Lillard (2021), "Initiated in 1907, Montessori pedagogy is the oldest surviving and most prevalent child-centered, constructivist education system in the world, practiced in over 500 public and thousands of private American schools and tens of thousands of schools around the world." Chapter 7 serves as a resource for educators, researchers, school administrators, families, policymakers, and anyone who is curious about Montessori education and its national and global influence. This chapter charts the constellation of organizations and initiatives that serve and uphold the Montessori community.

Welcome. May your reading influence your thinking about children's incredible capacity to absorb and engage with all that is made available through Montessori education.

CHAPTER 2

Overview of Montessori Education

DR. MARIA MONTESSORI

Maria Montessori, an educational theorist, held many identities over her lifetime: physician, women's rights activist, researcher, and scholar. As early as 1911, newsreels and articles published in popular magazines provided images of her work with children, leading people from around the world to attend her speaking engagements and trainings so they might replicate Montessori classrooms in their own communities. Highlights from her professional timeline between 1899 and 1951 demonstrate the influence and reach of her work (Association Montessori Internationale [AMI], n.d.-f). As a sought-after speaker, Montessori often engaged with dignitaries such as Alexander Graham Bell; his wife, Mabel Bell; U.S. President Wilson's daughter Margaret Woodrow Wilson; Queen Margharita of Italy; Queen Victoria of England; Anna Freud; and Mahatma Gandhi (Moretti, 2022; Perry, 2024). She sold out presentations at Carnegie Hall in New York, lectured at universities, and spoke passionately in support of children at the League of Nations in Geneva, the Sorbonne in Paris, and the General Conference of UNESCO in Florence. Montessori classrooms opened in major cities across the globe: Boston, New York, Paris, Vienna, and Amsterdam, among others. Trainings to prepare new Montessori teachers were held in Milan, the Netherlands, Barcelona, Dublin, and India. Her books were translated into multiple languages. Yet, despite the global recognition, even now, more than a century after the Montessori method was introduced to the world, she remains either a misrepresented educational theorist or one who is completely removed from history.

To better understand her vision of the Montessori method, a brief history lesson is required. Context matters, especially when we consider the intersection of her many achievements and the influence of historical events experienced in her lifetime.

As a young woman, Montessori publicly denounced hardships that impacted the lives of women and young children across Europe, as noted in her speech at the International Women's Congress in Berlin (1896). She focused on "liberty and social equality for women including equal pay and the right to vote. She prodded women to use their intellectual ability to solve social problems . . . (She) spoke out against the miserable working conditions for women and children in factories, opposed child labor, and advocated for peace and social reform"

(Cunningham, 2017, p. 29). For Montessori, inadequate education was the root of these social issues. She envisioned the power of education to improve social outcomes in communities, while also serving as a tool to forge a path toward global peace.

> She knew that for there to be real peace, there must be harmony among people. She saw the commonality of our humanness as the uniting factor in the face of the diversity found throughout the earth. "Preventing conflict is the work of politics; establishing peace is the work of education" (Brussels, 1936). Montessori saw her role as an educator as critical to creating the more peaceful world she desired. And it was for her work as a scientist, child advocate, and peace activist that Dr. Montessori was nominated for the Nobel Peace Prize three times in 1949, 1950, and 1951. (Cunningham, 2017, p. 21)

Soon after completing medical school, Montessori assumed the task of caring for young children in a classroom built in the basement of a new housing development in San Lorenzo, Italy. In this underresourced neighborhood sitting on the outskirts of Rome, she opened the first Children's House (Casa de Bambini) in 1907. And it was here that she developed a pedagogy—a scientific approach to teaching—that included specific materials and instructional approaches for children between the ages of 3 and 6. It's important to note that in the early 1900s, there were no early learning standards nor any recognized developmental milestones to inform her work with children. Rather, it was her direct study of the children in her care that informed her pedagogy. By using methodical observations learned during medical school and offering materials developed by earlier theorists, Montessori used the classroom as her scientific laboratory, and the children's responses were her living data.

With the growing success of her work with 3-to-6-year-old children, Montessori was asked to extend the pedagogy with older children, but she felt strongly that she needed to first look at the extraordinary transformations that occurred during the first 3 years of life (Honegger, 2023). Later, she expanded her approach to include elementary-age children along with principles developed for secondary education (AMI, n.d.-f; Duffy & Duffy, 2016). Unlike many of her contemporaries, Montessori created an educational system linking all phases of human development, from conception through early adulthood (Lnenickovä, 2015).

> The human personality is essentially one during the successive stages of its development. Yet, whatever human being we consider, and at whatever age, whether children in the primary school, adolescents, youths or adults, all start by being children, all then grow from childhood to manhood or womanhood without changing the unity of their persons. If the human personality is one at all stages of its development, we must conceive of a principle of education which has regard for all stages. (Montessori, 1955/1989, p. 7)

Her unconventional approach to teaching and learning was rooted in novel concepts such as liberty, freedom, and choice in the classroom. The emphasis is on Montessori education as a preparation for life that also supports readiness for academics. Montessori's view of the child and how to best meet their developmental needs—what she described as their human potential—were influenced by her work in the classroom. For further context, she was also influenced by life events such as living through two World Wars, a fascist regime that dominated her country, and her subsequent internment in India along with her son, Mario. Collectively, these events influenced Montessori's belief about the purpose of education. Education was more than a transfer of relevant cultural knowledge to a new generation. She envisioned a new world—even as her world was ravaged by politics and war. She boldly imagined a new existence where the primary outcomes of Montessori education would be a path to shared reverence and stewardship of our world, and a means for all citizens to learn to live collaboratively and thrive in peace.

THE LEARNER: HUMAN DEVELOPMENT AND FLOURISHING

Child development, "the study of the persistent, cumulative, and progressive changes in the physical, cognitive, and social emotional development of children and adolescents" (McDevitt & Ormrod, 2013, p. 4), is foundational to Montessori education. Grounded in over a century of deep theoretical roots, the pedagogy maintains a lens of children's learning and development within the cultural and linguistic context of where the classroom is situated. Montessori's extensive observations of children at work and play in her schools informed the materials she designed and the instructional approaches used by teachers. Children revealed particularly sensitive periods, or what today may be referenced as developmental milestones. "Critical and sensitive periods—time windows in which experience-related developmental transitions must or can most readily occur—create a temporal mapping of anticipated early childhood exposures that guide the timing and sequencing of developmental change" (National Academies of Sciences, Engineering, and Medicine, 2015, p. 59). The American Montessori Society (n.d.-a) describes sensitive periods as "times during human development when children are biologically ready and receptive to acquiring a specific skill or ability and are therefore particularly sensitive to stimuli that promote the development of that skill."

Yet, even with research-informed stages of children's development, there is often great variation in exactly when children speak, learn, grow, or reason out thoughts. The National Association for the Education of Young Children (2022) described these variations as "waves of development rather than stages" (p. 36) to highlight the individualized nature of children's development, rather than fixed expectations or boundaries. Each child uses their experiences to "build ideas about the world through a slow process of construction. They do not passively absorb information and ideas. They transform what they see and hear into something that is uniquely meaningful to them" (Levin, 2013, p. 13). These variations in learners' development are effectively managed in Montessori classrooms by implementing curricular and instructional approaches that are developmentally appropriate across multiple years. Unlike conventional classrooms that separate children by a single year (e.g., the Pre-K classroom for 4-year-olds, the 2nd-grade classroom), Montessori classrooms are designed to respond to the needs of students across a 3- or 6-year developmental span:

- Infants (*nido*) and toddlers in 0–3 classrooms
- Preschool age (*casa*) children in 3–6 classrooms
- Elementary-age children in 6–12 classrooms
- Adolescents in 12–18 classrooms

Depending on staffing requirements of individual Montessori schools, the 6-year age span noted in elementary and adolescent classrooms is also structured as Elementary I (6–9) and Elementary II (9–12), and 12–15 (middle school) and 15–18 (high school) classrooms. This model is responsive to all learners. As an example, when children have mastered an area of study or curricular content in a Montessori classroom, they can effortlessly move to material that conventional education might recognize as beyond grade-level expectations. The multiple-year age span allows students the grace of additional time to internalize learning and master new content beyond a scripted schedule.

Contemporary research conducted by the National Research Council (NRC) and the Institute of Medicine (IOM) in 2000 reviewed an extensive multidisciplinary compendium of studies to investigate the complexities of human development. During a child's early years, foundational brain architecture is dependent on genetics and the steady stream of experiences from their environment, as well as the reciprocal interactions children have with the adults in their lives.

> Children rapidly develop foundational capabilities on which subsequent development builds. In addition to their remarkable linguistic and cognitive gains, they exhibit dramatic progress in their emotional, social, regulatory, and moral capacities. All of these critical dimensions of early development are intertwined, and each requires focused attention. (NRC & IOM, 2000, p. 5)

See Table 2.1 for a list of five key concepts regarding children's development outlined by the Center for the Developing Child at Harvard University.

Learner-centered education offers curriculum and instruction that are "the proper level of difficulty in order to be and to remain motivating: tasks that are too easy become boring; tasks that are too difficult cause frustration. . . . (Students feel they) are contributing something to others . . . they see the usefulness of what they are learning and when they can use that information to do something that has an impact on others—especially their local community" (Bransford et al., 2000, p. 61). Educators play a pivotal role in learner-centered classrooms. Content is not recited to students; rather, educators help students construct their own

Table 2.1. The Science of Early Childhood Development

1. **Brains are built over time, from the bottom up.** The stability or fragility of the brain's architecture is dependent on the quality of early experiences. In the early years, 700 new neural connections are formed every second and will inform later learning, health, and behavior.
2. **The interactive influences on genes and experience shape the developing brain.** Serve-and-return, the positive interactive engagements between children and the adults in their environment, highly influences brain development. When these interactions are unreliable or negative, the brain's architecture does not form as expected and can lead to learning disparities.
3. **The brain's capacity for change decreases with age.** Early plasticity means that it's more effective to influence brain development during known "sensitive periods" than it is to rewire brain circuitry in later adult years.
4. **Cognitive, emotional, and social capacities are inextricably intertwined throughout the life course.** When we focus on children's social-emotional well-being, we set the stage for later cognitive skills. All domains of development, emotional and physical health, social skills, cognition, and language skills, are all foundational for school success and later competency in the workplace and community.
5. **Toxic stress damages development brain architecture, which can lead to lifelong problems in learning, behavior, and physical and mental health.** Unrelenting stress caused by extreme poverty, abuse, or severe maternal depression can negatively impact brain development. However, some stress can be mitigated by the presence of supportive adults who add a buffering protection to the architecture of the developing brain.

Adapted from: *In Brief: The Science of Early Childhood Development*, from the National Scientific Council on the Developing Child (2007)

meaning and make connections between new information and content that's been previously mastered. Learner-centered educators actively seek to understand the knowledge, skills, attitudes, and beliefs that their students bring to the classroom. They engage students by linking new content to their interests and passions. And instruction is presented as "well-organized bodies of knowledge that support planning and strategic thinking . . . (and educators hold the belief that) children are capable of sophisticated levels of thinking and reasoning when they have the knowledge necessary to support these activities" (Bransford et al., 2000, p. 138).

Montessori education is far more than unique learning materials; it is an approach to teaching and learning that supports children's development. Montessori proposed that her pedagogy would lead to human flourishing and a renewed humankind inclusive of our similarities and interconnectedness. Through decades of contemporary studies in neuroscience, we can now confirm what Montessori discovered more than a century ago through her own observations of children—what happens in these early years and beyond influences not only children's development, but the degree to which they will experience a prosperous and sustainable society. These educational outcomes are also a hallmark feature of human flourishing. Flourishing, described by VanderWeele (2024) is "the relative attainment of a state in which all aspects of a person's life are good including the contexts in which that person lives" (p. 3). In the landmark Global Flourishing Study (Gallup, 2025), researchers from Harvard and Baylor University, along with social scientists from Gallup, sought to answer one of life's most enduring questions: What contributes to a life well lived? They examined flourishing through a holistic lens that encompassed not just life dimensions, such as health or happiness, but also considered the contexts in which the individual lived. Their study of over 207,000 participants from 22 countries measured flourishing across six domains: happiness and life satisfaction, mental and physical health, meaning and purpose, character and virtue, close social relationships, and financial and material stability. To expand on elements of this study, Montessori education and character development (Duckworth, 2025) are aligned throughout this book. Specifically, character development is introduced as one theoretical model outlined in the next section and further discussed in Chapters 3, 4, 5, and 6.

THREE THEORETICAL MODELS OF HUMAN DEVELOPMENT

Over the course of her 50-year career, Montessori outlined a comprehensive plan to support children's learning and development. This section begins with an overview of her approach to observation as a tool to better understand children's development. Two contemporary theorists are also introduced, Uri Bronfenbrenner and Angela Duckworth. Uri Bronfenbrenner's work highlights the interactions between the child, the adult, and the environment through the Bioecological Model of Montessori Education: A Living System. The model has been adapted to consider the interactions between the child and the Montessori classroom from birth through adolescence. Angela Duckworth's research in character development also aligns with Montessori's pedagogy. Using the Strengths of Heart, Mind, and Will framework, connections are made to Montessori's Grace and Courtesy lessons that support skills students learn so they may be independent thinkers who engage in harmonious relationships with others.

Maria Montessori—Observations and Planes of Development

Observation—the act of closely watching, noting, and analyzing—was foundational to Dr. Montessori's scientific approach to understanding children's learning and development. Using clinical observation skills developed during her medical training, she later trained teachers in the importance of recognizing patterns in children's engagement in the classroom. Educators noted what materials children selected to work with and the length of time they devoted to each activity, and she formed an overall impression of their engagement and concentration in the classroom throughout the day (O'Shaughnessy, 2016a).

A Montessori teacher's observations are more than anecdotal notes of classroom happenings. They become data and evidence that are then analyzed to inform instructional decisions implemented in the days ahead. Observations create the path to individualized learning.

> The necessity for observing the children and anticipating their needs becomes of increased importance to a classroom environment where individual work allows a number of children to be engaging in different activities simultaneously under the direction of one teacher. The art of observation is a learned one. In classroom situations where the teacher is the active element and the children are passive, it is not important for a teacher to watch the children, as it is she determines what will be taught, when it will be taught, how it will be taught, and what gratifications will be forthcoming for the subject matter properly learned. In a Montessori classroom, however, extreme delicacy must be exercised by the teacher to anticipate needs, as well as to reinforce these needs when a child appears to be having difficulty. Therefore, there are rules for the observation of children which are extremely important for the teacher, so that she may have them well in hand. (Rambusch, 1962/2012, p. 94)

These rules for observation follow an iterative cycle that includes gathering objective information through multiple observational snapshots recorded throughout a child's day, organizing and reflecting on the observation data, and then interpreting the results. The observation cycle culminates with appropriate next steps in supporting children's learning and the cycle begins anew (O'Shaughnessy, 2016b).

Montessori viewed human development as a pathway to adulthood through four distinct stages, known as the Four Planes of Development. Her observations of children, the materials she developed, and her pedagogy were designed to support each period of development and its specific milestones of growth. These planes were then aligned to the following Montessori multi-age classroom configurations:

- Infancy, the first plane of development, takes place between birth through 6 years of age. Children experience an incredible period of growth, demonstrating sensitive periods for language, order, repetition, independence, and movement, among others. Montessori referenced children's "absorbent mind" at this stage, as they're able to take in, or absorb, knowledge from the environment around them without full conscious intent. Montessori learning environments are identified as infants (birth—approximate 12 months), toddlers (12 months—2.5 years), and early childhood (3–6 years).
- Childhood is the second plane, from 6 to 12 years of age. There is a greater focus on students' social development, abstract reasoning, and nurturing of their sense of responsibility. Children have more contact with the wider community and, through the power of imagination and stories, expand their consciousness of the world. Language continues to be an important area of development as vocabulary related to biology,

history, botany, math, and more increases and extends to children's reading and writing. Montessori classrooms include lower elementary (6–9 years) and upper elementary (9–12 years).
- Adolescence is the third plane of development. It occurs from 12 to 18 years of age as adolescents enter sensitive periods of social consciousness and their emotional skills continue to grow, as does their economic/fiscal independence through experiences implemented both inside and outside the Montessori classroom. At this stage, students want to fully explore areas of personal interest and engage in real-world experiences that may inform future career opportunities. Montessori classrooms include middle school (12–15 years) and high school (16–18 years).
- Maturity represents the fourth plan, where young adults from 18 to 24 years of age move into adulthood. Montessori also outlined principles of learning in higher education for this plane of development. (AMI, n.d.-f; Duffy & Duffy, 2016)

Developmental standards outlining specific milestones for a given age group did not yet exist in the early 1900s, but Montessori's Planes of Development framework outlined the materials and activities that engaged children for extended periods of time. Silvana Quattrocchi Montanaro (1991) quoted Montessori from a 1931 lecture where she stated, "In order to understand the child so as to be able to educate him, we must first know life in its entirety" (p. 5). We can infer that it's not sufficient to know about children's development for a single age group or grade level. For example, a kindergarten teacher would of course benefit from knowledge of the cognitive, social-emotional, and physical development of the 5-year-old children in their classroom, but Montessori proposed that teachers would be best prepared when they had deep knowledge of development across the life continuum. This is particularly important because Montessori educators work with children across a minimum of a 3-year age span. Having a wide range of knowledge of children's development allows Montessori educators to be inclusive of students who have not yet mastered foundational skills for their age group, as well as those who are ready to move beyond the 3-year curriculum.

Lessons in Montessori classrooms are offered, not imposed. Children are not underestimated, nor are they required to respond to predetermined timelines. Rather, educators follow children's developmental trajectories, demonstrating that "education cannot individualize teaching—education can only individualize learning" (Sackett, 2016, p. 6). Regardless of the age of the child, agency is visible in Montessori classrooms. Agency is "the personal capacity to act and make free and informed choices to pursue a specific goal—it empowers [individuals] to actively participate in and engage with the world around them" (UNICEF & Gallup, 2021, p. 38). Agency is a necessary skill to build if one goal of education is to prepare students to become active participants in their community. Therefore, environments are tailored to individual learning, and educators facilitate human development by creating "environments, relationships, [and] activities that support and enhance the person's understanding of the world and ability to function in it" (Shelton, 2019, p. 12).

Uri Bronfenbrenner—Bioecological Theory of Development

Uri Bronfenbrenner (1979), like Montessori, viewed human development through the lens of active engagement in the environment. He defined development as

> the process through which the growing person acquires a more extended, differentiated, and valid conception of the ecological environment, and becomes motivated and able to engage in activities that reveal the properties of, sustain, or restructure that environment at levels of similar or greater complexity in form and content (p. 27).

For Bronfenbrenner, "the person exists in a system of relationships, roles, activities, and settings, all interconnected" (Shelton, 2019, p. 10). Using a series of nested circles, he designed the bioecological model to map the many influences on children's development. Bronfenbrenner, like Montessori, believed that "humans are not only a product of but also a producer of their own development" (Hayes et al., 2023, p. 17). It's a valuable education tool, especially in learner-centered classrooms, as it helps educators map the many contextual factors that impact their students. What students experience outside the classroom is just as influential as what happens within the classroom environment.

Visually, the bioecological model is much like a Russian matryoshka doll. Similar to the series of wooden figures, each that separates to reveal an increasingly smaller wooden figure within it, Bronfenbrenner's bioecological model is represented through a series of nested circles. The innermost circle, what he called microsystems, represents the child's immediate environment and earliest influences: their home, community, and classroom. Within these environments, there are activities and individuals, such as family members, caretakers, and other children. To Bronfenbrenner, learning does not occur when information is dispensed to a child. Rather, it's the transactional nature of a child interacting with materials or activities in their environment, as well as the exchanges between other individuals, that best supports development.

To better reflect Montessori education, Bronfenbrenner's bioecological model has been adapted to the Bioecological Model of Montessori Education: A Living System (see Figure 2.1). Similar to Bronfenbrenner's model, the Montessori adaptation begins with the innermost sphere of the nested system. The child is situated at the center along with family members in the home, caregivers from their school, and other influences from their community (microsystems). When the child and family become engaged in Montessori education, the sphere extends to include the many interactions that occur between home and school—what Bronfenbrenner identified as mesosystems. The model then extends to include indirect influences on the child represented as the Montessori Constellation. This layer of the model,

Figure 2.1. Bioecological Model of Montessori Education: A Living System

Bioecological Model of Montessori Education
A Living System

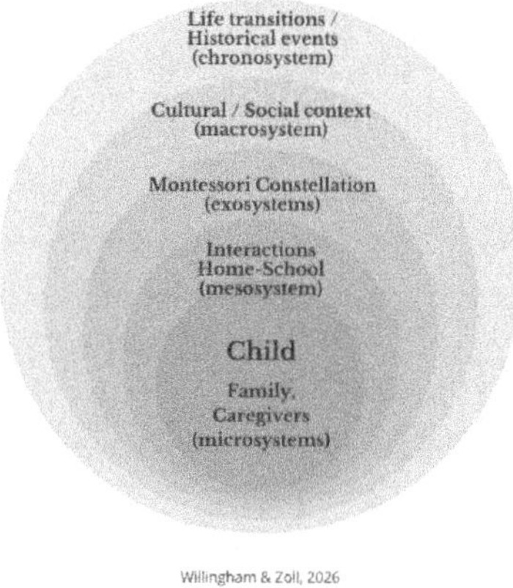

Thompson-Willingham, T., & Zoll, S. (2026). *Implementing the Montessori Method.* Teachers College Press.

referred to as exosystems, highlights the many outside systems that provide indirect support of children's experiences in Montessori classrooms. Organizations at this level of the model are less visible and do not engage in direct, everyday contact like that between a child and their teacher. Rather, this level represents the many organizations that support teachers, classroom environments, and schools to maintain the highest level of integrity to the Montessori approach to teaching and learning. The Montessori Constellation includes organizations that serve as membership and professional development hubs, those that lead teacher preparation, develop Montessori materials, and conduct research and advocacy efforts, among others. Though these organizations certainly influence the child, the child does not directly interact with them (Hayes et al., 2023, p. 15). Additional information about the Montessori Constellation will be discussed in Chapter 7.

The Montessori model also considers the child's cultural and social context (macrosystem). This includes the sociocultural beliefs a community holds about education and the rights and responsibilities of children (Hayes et al., 2023). Finally, the outermost circle includes historical events and life transitions children experience (chronosystem), including transitions they make between each age level of Montessori classrooms. This book primarily focuses on the meso- and exosystems adapted from Bronfenbrenner's ecological model to demonstrate the influence of Montessori education on children's development.

Within this Montessori ecosystem, the learner is an active participant within an interconnected system of relationships, roles, activities, and settings, all designed

Figure 2.2. Montessori Mesosystem

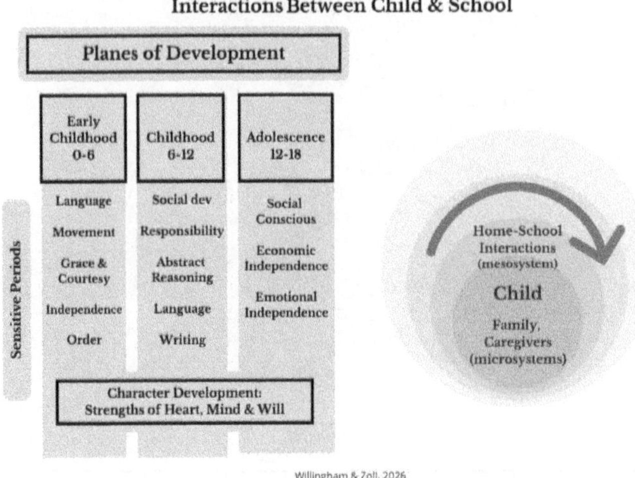

to meet their developmental needs. Ultimately, what occurs within this ecosystem informs who they will be as a friend, coworker, parent, community member, and global citizen. Figure 2.2 highlights the interactions between the child and their Montessori school experience (mesosystem) represented by Montessori's Planes of Development, sensitive periods, and character development further elaborated in the next section.

It is important to keep these early experiences in mind because as a child enters a Montessori classroom, they bring with them a wealth of knowledge influenced by the settings and relationships they've encountered in their young lives—the people and activities in their home, their community, the language(s) they hear, the culture they are immersed in, and the religious organizations they attend. These elements of living have informed children's development and are the funds of knowledge they bring with them as they enter the Montessori classroom at any age level.

Bronfenbrenner and Montessori both considered development at the level of the learner and recognized that development is greatly influenced by a host of contextual factors, not all of which are positive. The Integrative Model, developed by Cynthia Garcia Coll and her colleagues (1996), extends Bronfenbrenner's ecosystem by considering detrimental outside influences on human development, including economic insufficiency, health access and health consequences, and poor housing, as well as the negative impacts of racism, prejudice, and discrimination. However, education that is responsive to development and embedded in a culture of belonging can be one way to mitigate negative macro-influences. According to Hayes et al., "A welcoming learning environment invites and accommodates individual differences in abilities, skills, and competencies, including an emphasis on engaging with and across different age groups. Rich learning environments reflect diversity in family types and differences in socio-economic class and culture" (2023, p. 103). And rich learning environments invite students to actively participate in the classroom so that they may construct an understanding of themselves and of their world.

Angela Duckworth—Character Development

The human capacity for learning is immense! Consider how knowledge has propelled the growth of science and technology just in your own lifetime. Not only have we sequenced human DNA, but we can now edit that sequence to individualize medical interventions, as well as improve agricultural and biotechnology practices through a tool called CRISPR (Asmamaw & Belay, 2021). And we're at the threshold of artificial intelligence (AI) applications so astounding that we cannot yet fathom their reach or implications for human society. Families invest time and resources to ensure their children's readiness and success in these emerging fields. Knowledge-building has long been equated with career-building. But should education only be knowledge-building?

Parker Palmer (1998) passionately warned that school systems were "dispensing facts at the expense of meaning, information at the expense of wisdom. The price is a school system that alienates and dulls us, that graduates young people who have had no mentoring in the questions that both enliven and vex the human spirit." Mahatma Gandhi went even further, labeling education without character as one of seven social sins that held the power to end humanity from within society, rather than from outside forces. Knowledge has the power to improve life on an incredible scale, but knowledge without character has the potential to inflict harm and control.

As described earlier, Montessori education is a comprehensive curriculum, including both knowledge- and character-building experiences. Young children are introduced to Grace and Courtesy lessons, learning relationship skills and respectful interactions within the classroom community (Chapter 4). Later they'll learn about the needs of humankind and gain respect for the growth of societies throughout history via the Great Stories (Chapter 5) and then learn to apply these knowledge- and character-building skills through these real-life situations in community settings (Chapter 6).

This learning has been aligned to Angela Duckworth's research in character development. According to Duckworth (2025), character

> refers to ways of thinking, acting, and feeling that benefit others as well as ourselves. Character is plural—encompassing strengths of heart, mind, and will. Strengths of heart (such as gratitude and kindness) enable harmonious relationships with other people. Strengths of mind (such as curiosity and creativity) enable independent thinking. Strengths of will (such as grit and self-control) enable us to achieve goals.

Children's character is strengthened through their agency in the classroom. "Character consists of a capacity and tendency toward fully expressing agency, which . . . consists of choosing for oneself active work that involves normative standards and persistently engaging in that work" (Fierson, 2023, p. 35). In addition to freedom of choice and movement in the classroom, students simultaneously experience responsibility for their choices and develop mutual respect toward others. Montessori believed children's character was often weakened by school procedures such as punishment or minimizing student decision-making. Instead, she observed children who experienced joy and peace when engaged in self-selected uninterrupted activity. This became the foundation of character development that was later extended through Grace and Courtesy lessons, where children learned to "properly address one another, resolve conflicts, or negotiate situations requiring respect . . . (and) taking on potential classroom conflicts as problem-solving opportunities" (Fierson, 2023, p. 76).

Duckworth's character development curriculum, outlined in Table 2.2, notes 15 character traits, eight of which are discussed in this book. Character attributes are not found in a single age group. Rather, any can be practiced (or, as Duckworth describes, modeled, celebrated, and enabled) in a developmentally appropriate way at any stage of human development.

David Brooks, in his 2025 opinion piece in *The New York Times*, "The Character Building Tool-Kit," shared his belief that "character is destiny and that moral formation is at the center of any healthy society . . . [To Brooks] people's characters are primarily formed when they live within coherent moral ecologies."

Table 2.2. Character Development—Strengths of Heart, Mind, and Will

Domain	Character Notes	Chapter
Strengths of Heart	Gratitude—appreciating what you've been given	*Application in Chapter 5, Elementary (6–12) Classroom
	Kindness—action or speech intended to help others	*Application in Chapter 4, Preschool (3–6) Classroom
	Honesty—telling, and not hiding, the truth	
	Purpose—commitment to making a meaningful contribution to the world	*Application in Chapter 3, Infant-Toddler (0–3) Classroom
	Social Intelligence—the ability to connect with other people	*Application in Chapter 3, Infant-Toddler (0–3) Classroom
	Emotional Intelligence—understanding your feelings and using them wisely	

Domain	Character Notes	Chapter
Strengths of the heart *"encourage relating to other people in positive ways. They are interpersonal—either in the sense of an ethical and loving posture toward friends, family, and close others or in the sense of civic virtue, including our duty to our neighbors, our country, and the world beyond our borders" (Duckworth, 2024).*		
Strengths of Mind	Curiosity—wanting to know more	*Application in Chapter 4, Preschool (3–6) Classroom
	Judgment—getting as close as possible to the right answer	*Application in Chapter 6, Adolescent (12–18) Classroom
	Decision-Making—choosing wisely	
	Creativity—thinking of novel solutions	
	Intellectual Humility—recognizing the limitations of your own knowledge	
Strengths of mind *"encourage active and open-minded thinking. In this day and age, these intellectual virtues may seem in short supply. All the more reason to intentionally support their development" (Duckworth, 2024).*		
Strengths of Will	Growth Mindset—believing you can improve your abilities	
	Proactivity—taking initiative	*Application in Chapter 6, Adolescent (12–18) Classroom
	Self-Control—doing what's best despite short-term temptations	
	Grit—passion and perseverance for long-term goals	*Application in Chapter 5, Elementary (6–12) Classroom
Strengths of will *"encourage the achievement of goals. These are intrapersonal insofar as they enable you to triumph over self-doubt, indecision, inertia, and other obstacles to a desired future" (Duckworth, 2024).*		

Adapted from Duckworth, 2024; Park et al., 2017.

Character development can be supported by institutions like schools that adhere to certain standards and lead with clear goals and a moral mission. It requires schools to prioritize who their students become over their career aspirations. Brooks ends his comments with a reminder that our democracy imposed "greater moral demands on the citizenry than any other form of government. [Our founders] were intent on building morally formative institutions that would produce such citizens.

We've kind of dropped the ball on this over the past few generations. But signs of hope are everywhere to be found." Montessori also found signs of hope. A peaceful world would be realized through education, and it would begin with the child.

THE ADULT IN THE CLASSROOM

Teaching is complex. Yet it is often the least visible component of Montessori education. We can see the didactic materials. We can also observe the children and their interactions in the classroom. What is less visible are the discrete actions of a Montessori educator. They conduct observations with stealth-like precision. And rather than gathering all children to deliver whole-group instruction, children are primarily invited to individual or small-group lessons designed to meet their developmental needs. Then, based on in-the-moment decision-making conducted during instruction, students will either progress to new material or review lessons as needed to master content.

Teachers in Montessori settings are referred to as "guides." The process of learning is an active one for the child, and the role of the adult is to support that ongoing endeavor. In this book, *guide* and *educator* are used interchangeably. The educator's role, then, is to both guide children to optimal learning experiences and to model the appropriate use of Montessori materials. Montessori characterized the didactic materials as another "teacher" in the classroom (Orem, 1974). Didactic materials in a Montessori classroom are

> a systematic array of objects resembling learning games, each of which is carefully designed to impart particular learnings. They are materials of wood, metal, cardboard, etc. for sensory education, mathematics, language, science, and other areas. The materials are usually manipulable and contain a 'control of error' enabling the learner to work alone successfully. (Orem, 1974, p. 28)

As an example, if a child works with the Knobbed Cylinders—a wooden block holding 10 cylinders of different widths and/or heights—the block is designed to hold only one cylinder accurately. The child will recognize when an error is made when any remaining cylinders do not fit in the open spaces left in the block. Since many of the Montessori materials have this built-in feature, the control of error provides immediate and tangible feedback to students. Once they receive an initial lesson, they are then free to work with the material as frequently and for as much time they choose, working toward mastery of a particular skill—all with minimal or no adult supervision.

International membership organizations, such the Association Montessori Internationale (AMI), the American Montessori Society (AMS), and the International Montessori Council (IMC), have set standards for educators who teach in their accredited schools. Educators who work in AMI-recognized schools are tasked with supporting young children in their

> process of self-development. They are foremost an observer, unobtrusively yet carefully monitoring each child's development, recognising and interpreting each child's needs. The teacher provides a link between the child and the prepared environment, introducing the child to each piece of equipment when he or she is ready in a precise, clear and enticing way. The most important attribute of a Montessori teacher is the love and respect she holds for each child's total being. (Association Montessori Internationale, n.d.-a)

The American Montessori Society outlined the role of Montessori educators in their School Accreditation Standards (AMS, 2023, Standards 3.20–3.30, p. 5), requiring that they demonstrate sound research-based teaching practices, along with internalizing core beliefs of Montessori philosophy, such as fostering independence, recognizing children's sensitive periods, planes of development, and their intrinsic motivation.

And the International Montessori Council (IMC) in their School Accreditation Handbook (2024, Quality 5: The Montessori Teacher Is, p. 13) details the teacher's role as authoritative, one who is firm at the edges and empathetic at the center; an observer who is capable of inferring children's intentions through observation; a resource the children can turn to for help in acquiring knowledge; and a model who embodies the behaviors and dispositions that support children's development.

These guidelines highlight Montessori's focus on the role of the adult in the classroom in three areas: (1) the preparation of the teacher, (2) the preparation of the classroom, and (3) the educator's role as curator of classroom culture.

Preparation of the Educator

To meet the needs of all children, current Montessori guides are advised to complete a training program recognized by the Montessori Accreditation Council for Teacher Education (MACTE). Trainings prioritize educators having a deep knowledge of human development. There is a focus on children's thinking, understanding how they process information, and how they grow and learn over a 3-to-6-year span so they can interpret children's actions along a continuum of development. This information "is essential for planning curriculum; designing, sequencing, and pacing activities; diagnosing student learning needs; organizing the classroom; and teaching social and academic skills" (Horowitz et al., 2005, p. 88). Foundational knowledge of development informs all instructional decisions the teacher will make for each child.

> Montessori educators are the driving force behind the transformative power of Montessori education. Becoming a Montessori teacher is a journey that requires time, dedication, critical thinking, reflection, and a deep understanding of Montessori philosophy beyond the use of materials. The transformation of the adult is a central tenet of teacher preparation, calling for self-awareness, self-reflection, character

> development, and care of one's emotional health. It encourages an internal audit of one's biases, openness to differences, and respect for the potential of *all* children. (Shivji & Taliaferro Lofquist, 2024, p. 187)

Montessori guides conduct ongoing observations to document children's interactions and learning in the classroom. Their observations serve as data in record keeping systems as they monitor lessons offered to, and ultimately mastered by, the children (Zoll et al., 2023). Observation skills are refined through ongoing practice over the course of educators' careers. They carefully track lessons presented to students, noting when follow-up activities are needed. Unlike conventional classrooms where curriculum is scripted, dictating the weekly delivery of lessons to the whole class, Montessori educators follow each child to determine their readiness for a given lesson. Implementing an individualized curriculum requires that Montessori educators analyze their student observation data to inform instructional "next steps" mapping learning across a developmental continuum.

According to Morgan Herman and Saylor, "In her discussion of observation in education, Montessori emphasizes the distinction between seeing and true observation, highlighting that perception, rooted in knowledge, is crucial . . . our task is to know the intricacies of child development and overlay that knowledge onto the individual children" (2023, pp. 22–23). This requires educators have both a deep understanding of child development along with a working knowledge of all Montessori materials relevant to the multiyear curriculum of their certification. They understand the purpose of each material and how to introduce and model its use with children, while also developing keen timing, sensing when to offer support or remove barriers that might impede children's success.

Preparation of the Classroom

The trained Montessori guide understands that the classroom environment *is* the curriculum. This is unlike conventional schools that use commercially published curriculum outlined for domains of learning (math, science, English language arts, etc.). When Montessori educators complete their training, they have (re)created a multiyear curriculum covering all domains of learning aligned to their level. For example, training programs require preservice teachers to review and practice with each piece of classroom material alongside their instructor. Much attention is given to the delivery of the lesson and to the specific language used. They will then rewrite each lesson plan that will be added to their personal curriculum binders, which will be used as a teaching resource throughout their careers. Though many training programs now offer preprinted lesson handouts, those that adhere to Montessori's original teaching still require educators to write and illustrate each lesson by hand as part of their teacher training. This reflects Montessori's belief that the hand is a companion to the mind (Montessori 1967/1995), and the exercise of handwriting each lesson reinforces teachers' learning, a concept supported by current research (Van der Weel & Van der Meer, 2024).

Ultimately, educators enter classrooms prepared to implement the Montessori curriculum. The materials have remained fundamentally constant over the last 100 years, allowing educators to focus on refining their classroom practice and learning environments. Unlike their conventional school colleagues, Montessori educators are not routinely required to learn and implement new curriculum and assessment tools. Instead, educators' precious time can be devoted to improving their work in the classroom so that they can meet the needs of all students.

Curator of Classroom Culture

The culture informs priorities and agreements upheld by all members of the classroom, making visible the beliefs and expectations defined by both students and educators. Culture includes the approach educators use to support students' love of learning, and their curiosity, independence, kindness, and respect for all living things. If the materials are the "what" of Montessori education, then culture is the "how" and "why" that define how members of the classroom will present themselves and how they will work together. This way of being in the classroom informs students' character development as they work toward realizing their human potential. As an example, a student may forget their responsibility to respect a classroom peer. This momentary lapse becomes a learning moment for the student as they repair an injured relationship, rather than an opportunity for the student to experience shame or punishment.

Montessori training begins with theory, but it's through teachers' direct experience in the classroom where culture is developed. An observer will witness how educators model, celebrate, and nurture students' development. Educators construct systems and rituals that keep the big picture in mind: Student choice, independence, organization, respect, and trust are constants in the classroom. They translate grand ideas to practical applications through expectations they set, by way of classroom routines and how the dynamics of classroom relationships are managed.

As mentioned earlier, educators place great emphasis on lesson delivery, highlighting points of interest to students (intentionally selecting two cubes, the smallest and the largest, to compare through sight and touch, for example). They isolate difficulties. The focus is on process in learning versus product in work, and mistakes are considered opportunities to reinforce learning. Classroom schedules include dedicated work periods where children's time is protected from extraneous events, allowing students to build concentration. And ongoing individualized lessons are prompted through invitations initiated by the adult or through the student's interests and requests.

What's not found in a Montessori classroom are forms of rewards or punishments, such as behavior charts or time-outs. Educators avoid assumptive language like "friends" or "challenging work," as children will decide who their friends are and what they consider challenging. Educators also refrain from offering judgments and unsolicited praise like "good job." Instead, they offer validation of children's effort and point out details they notice within the work ("Last week you read an entire chapter, but today I noticed you were also able to write a reflection about the character!"). In early childhood classrooms, worksheets or other printed assignments are not needed, nor are young children required to sit in a group circle for extended periods of time. In elementary classrooms, worksheets might be available as a follow-up to a lesson but are rarely assigned; rather, the students might create them as a way of extending their learning.

Without understanding the practice of fostering a Montessori culture, one might merely have a homey classroom with beautiful materials. Though there is agreement regarding core elements in Montessori education, as noted in the Montessori Essentials (MPPI, 2015), implementing a high-fidelity Montessori classroom requires a wider skill set. Montessori recognized the foundational importance of the adult. The human who is in service to the child's development must engage in ongoing reflection and refinement of their own practice—an essential component of the pedagogy. Additional expectations related to the educator's role in the Montessori classroom, specific to the age group they work with, are further explored in Chapters 3 through 6.

CHAPTER 3

Montessori 0–3 Environments

By the age of three the children have completely laid down the foundations of their personality as human beings. I hold that any reform of education must be based on the personality of man . . . and we must never forget that man begins his mental growth at birth, and pursues it with the greatest intensity during the first three years of life. To this period, more than any other, it is imperative to give active care. The child's dignity will appear in front of us in the measure to which we see in him the builder of our own minds, one guided by his inward teacher, who labors indefatigably in joy and happiness—following a precise timetable—at the work of constructing that greatest marvel of the universe—the human being.

—M. Montessori, *The Absorbent Mind*, 1989, pp. 4–9

TWO 0–3 CLASSROOM VIGNETTES

The first 1,000 days of a child's life, from the moment of conception through to the end of their second year of life, are a "period of maximum developmental plasticity, and therefore the period with the greatest potential to affect health and wellbeing over the life course" (Moore et al., 2017). These crucial early days are a short-lived window of opportunity to support children's lifelong ability to learn, grow, and thrive (1,000 Days, n.d.)

Knowing the importance of these early days in a young child's development, the following two vignettes offer a view into Montessori classrooms and care offered to infants and toddlers. It should be noted the arrangement of Montessori infant-toddler classrooms is largely dependent on local licensing regulations of care. These regulations reflect protocols addressing children's safety and early development. The youngest children, from 6 weeks through approximately their first birthday (or when they are able to walk), are enrolled in the infant or *nido* classroom. Nido, meaning nest in Italian, is the perfect description for the nurturing space designed for the youngest children. Once children are mobile, at approximately 12 months old, they are enrolled in toddler classrooms through 2.5 to 3 years of age. With this in mind, two classroom vignettes are provided to offer the reader additional context of children's development and what might be observed during a morning's activities with young children.

The Nido

It was 8:25 in the morning, and there were five children and three adults in the room. Was this the whole class? The adults in the room were on the floor, at eye level with the children, who had recently become steady on their feet and mostly stood or sat on the floor.

The room was not silent, but not loud either—the adult voices could be heard mainly offering single words or phrases as the children grunted, squealed, or made sounds that almost sounded like words but not quite. The adults used gestures along with language if offering guidance. One adult was handed a book by a child, and then the child plopped themself into the adult's lap. The adult proceeded to open the book and read it to the child. A nearby child listened too and repeated "boad, boad, boad." "That's right, that's a boat!" the adult replied.

The outside door opened, and a parent entered with a child in arms and a bag of belongings. "Good morning," an adult offered. "Good morning," the parent replied. A different adult standing nearby said hello to the child and reached out her arms. The child transferred easily, and the parent proceeded to put their child's belongings into a cupboard close by and their child's shoes down low, under a bench. At the child's prompting, the adult gently placed him on the floor within the gated area, and he looked around.

An adult nearby had unrolled a mat and selected a basket from a shelf. The new child approached and sat down. The adult took a drawstring bag out of the basket and, with four fingers inside, moved her hands apart to open it. "Pull," she said. The child watched and took the bag from the adult. He put his hand in the bag and asked. "Is there anything in there?" She looked, then replied, "Just your hand."

Next, a zippered pouch was pulled from the basket by the adult. As she pulled the tab, she said, "Pull." Then she turned it around, pulled the tab, and closed it. As she did, she narrated. "PULL." The child was still holding the bag with his hand in it, but he pulled it out, took the pouch from the adult, and zipped it intently. "PUH." The child was up and making his way over to a wooden frog and stick over by the wall. The child pointed and said, "Evy." The child looked at another adult—"Evy . . . Evy." The adult replied—"Oh, is that heavy, you think?" The child nodded and toddled over to the frog. He picked up the stick and hit the frog to make a noise. Perhaps thinking this deserved some time, he continued to hit the frog as it emits a noise. A little girl nearby started bouncing to the beat. They looked at each other and smiled. The adults were all smiling too. "That's it!" one of the adults said.

Meanwhile, another child had made their way to the mat and picked the last item, a wooden box, out of the basket and twisted the top to open it. Then the child twisted the top again to close it. This went on for a while and the child said, "Tiss . . . tiss . . . tiss." An adult close by replied, "Twist."

This free movement and following of interests were continuous for the now 10 children who arrived in the last 10 minutes, one at a time with the same routine. There were many things for the children to explore but the space was big and sparse. The space included a ball track, a pickler triangle, a mat with pillows, and shelves holding various puzzles, activities, and books. There were lots of little cardboard books that were spontaneously taken by a child to an adult to read or just used independently by children, who flipped the pages and browsed the pictures. Sometimes the children used words and sometimes they worked silently.

As the morning moved on and the children circulated from interest to interest, the adults were situated among them, offering language, tidying up, singing a little song, and reading a book. Occasionally, a child would take something from another child, and an adult would calmly and without changing tone, make a statement like, "Johnny is using the train right now; let's find the book with the train," thereby directing the child away to engage in the book.

At some point, tidying the room became more of the focus and an adult and a child or two transitioned to the snack/bed area. There were tables with small chairs set around each one. At each place sat a plate with toast and apple pieces. One adult walked around and offered metal cups filled with water to each child. The other two adults were sitting at the tables on the floor, helping as needed. One child in particular would get up with his toast in what seemed like an absent-minded way. The adult redirected them with a calm word and gesture to come sit back down. This happened three times. "We need to sit when we eat," she said. To another child, "Are you finished? We need to wash your face." They moved together to a bin that held damp washcloths scrunched into balls. Once used, the child put the washcloth into a bin of dirty cloths and then made their way over to the low sink to wash their hands. All of the items they needed were within reach and used well.

Just as smoothly as the last transition to snacktime had occurred, the transition from snack to face washing to diaper changing to going outside happened in stages for the children, but without waiting or the whole group having to do the same thing at the same time. The adults were not always with the same children. and they never spoke to each other about a plan; it just happened as if it were routine and each child was able to go at their own pace as they saw fit. A child who was not interested in going outside with their peers was able to lie in a bed and watch one of the adults tidy up the snack items and then go with them to wash dishes. Eventually, the adult enticed the child to go outside with the idea of blowing bubbles, and they went willingly. There were a lot of suggestive questions from the adult—"Shall we play in the sand box? Do you think there will be a game of tag?" and "No's' from the child in the process—but in the end, they could not resist the idea.

When the children went outside, it looked like it would rain and an adult offered this observation to the children. The children who were wearing socks sat down and removed them before they left the classroom. Outside, the children were joyous, exploring the many options—the sandbox, the slide, the mint leaves poking through the fence, the big trucks, and the tricycle. Their bare feet had access to an outdoor rug, cushioned mats, concrete, plush grass. One child went from one sensory experience to the next, wiggling their toes and slowly flapping their arms as an expression of pleasure. It began to drizzle, and three large umbrellas were subtly raised. The children mostly continued exploring, sometimes looking up and squinting. One boy was in the sandbox and noticed an ant beside him on the ground. He stopped and watched it wander for a while. An adult began singing a song about the rain quietly, and a few children came over to listen with their hands full of buckets and trucks.

Since there is such incredible change in children in the first 3 years of life, such as their increasing mobility between 1 and 2 years old, young toddlers are often separated from those who are not yet capable in this way. It is for safety as well as extending expectations of children for their abilities to do things on their own. As skills grow, independence does too! You can visualize the growth as you read the next vignette of the toddler classroom.

The Toddler Classroom

The room was home-like, with nooks and spaces seemingly for different purposes. The shelves were low—everything was within reach for the wee ones. It was practical and well-thought-out. One thing that stood out was that the plates, the trays, and the tools were child-sized versions of what adults would use. The class was noisy with young chatter and the sound of things dropping, chairs moving, and beneath it all, the low tone of adult voices—they were audible, but it wasn't possible to hear what they were saying without listening very carefully.

One child picked up a towel-like apron and popped it over her head as preparation for peeling and slicing a hard-boiled egg. She must have been around 2, with expertise in this task. Upon completion of preparing her snack, she could not wait to sit down at the snack table to eat it. Instead, she gobbled it up and then put everything back on the tray and on the shelf, in the blink of an eye.

At another table were two children who appeared to be sisters—possibly twins—sitting side by side, each with their own puzzle. They were the kind of puzzles where you push small sticks in holes to complete a design. When one finished, the other admired it and waited. Then, all at once, a coordinated effort began. They pushed and pulled the tray on which each puzzle sat until the swap was complete. Each child fulfilled their new task, and then when each had finished and glanced at the other's second endeavor, they carried the puzzles back to a shelf where they appeared to belong.

Across the room was a child—*was she washing dishes?* She found great joy in the noise of one dish hitting the others as she plopped it in the rinse sink. At this point, an adult subtly walked past to ensure the child's safety. Throughout the morning, this adult seemed to take on preparing the classroom for the children. I saw her quickly washing the egg peeler between uses and replacing towels when they went missing

One of the other adults was situated close to the bathroom setup, facilitating toileting and all the elements involved in that critical level of independence. Some children were dressed in cloth underwear on the bottom, and some were fully clothed, apparently determined by their stage of toileting awareness.

The lead guide interacted with students on the other side of the room. She was seated at a table with three other children, who all had their own work. One student in particular seemed a little younger than the rest. They were making a quiet whimpering sound and stayed close to the guide, and she accepted their need for closeness. She was engaged in a language exercise with another child seated to her right. The first child looked over their shoulder quietly, watching the lesson. When the language lesson ended, the guide reached for an activity from the shelf behind her and put it on the table to her left. She quietly invited the child to sit, using her words and her gestures. They did! She took one of the items out of the basket and laid it out in front. Still quietly mewing, the child finished pulling all the items out and purposefully arranged them. Then he sat looking at them. Another child to the left of that child asked if they could do that work. The guide asked the child if they were finished, and without a word, they put it all away, and the other child quickly reached for the activity.

A child from across the room came over and asked the guide if she would do animal work with him. She nodded and verbally responded "yes" and got up to join him. The young boy from the round table followed her, still making subtle quiet sounds. As the guide sat on the carpet to engage with the next child, the young one followed her and stood behind her. As he did, he noticed something on the shelf near him. It was an activity with photographs in a basket. He picked one up and burst wide open in the direction of the guide.

"SNOW!"

The guide turned to him with a warm smile that equaled his enthusiasm.

"It is!" she said.

THE INFANT-TODDLER IN THE 0–3 MONTESSORI CLASSROOM

The earliest days of human life have a profound influence on human development. Beginning from conception through the first few years of life, a child's "development proceeds at a pace exceeding that of any subsequent stage of life" (NRC & IOM, 2000, p. 4). This development spans all domains: language, cognition, physical, social, emotional, regulatory, and moral capabilities—quickly building foundational capacities that will inform subsequent development and growth.

In the book *From Neurons to Neighborhoods*, core concepts of child development were outlined by researchers from the National Research Council and the Institute of Medicine (NRC & IOM, 2000). Their work offers a framework highlighting the incredible capacities young children demonstrate from the earliest stages of their development. These concepts mirror many of the insights offered by Silvana Quattrocchi Montanaro, who is recognized for her work in revitalizing AMI's 0–3 training in the 1980s and carrying forward Montessori's vision for planning the care of infants and toddlers (see Table 3.1).

Children's development is shaped by their own biology, and is also influenced by home and caretaking environments, the quality of relationships, and child-rearing practices and beliefs of the adults who care for them. Young children are

Table 3.1. Comparison Chart—Early Child Development

From Neurons to Neighborhoods	Montessori Birth to–3
Core concepts of child development include: • Human development is shaped by a dynamic and continuous interaction between biology and experience. • Culture influences every aspect of human development and is reflected in childrearing beliefs and practices designed to promote healthy adaptation. • The growth of self-regulation is a cornerstone of early childhood development that cuts across all domains of behavior. • Children are active participants in their own development, reflecting the intrinsic human drive to explore and master one's environment. • The broad range of individual differences among young children often makes it difficult to distinguish normal variations and maturational delays from transient disorders and persistent impairment. • The development of children unfolds along individual pathways whose trajectories are characterized by continuities and discontinuities, as well as by a series of significant transitions. (NRC & IOM, 2000, 3–4)	• Each human being is born into the world with an immense potential. • Each human being has marvelous self-regulating mechanisms that are frequently prevented from working because of our interference in vital processes. • Each person close to a child is important and can be an "educator" because they could help in development, if they know what to do. • The period from 0 to 3 years of age is one in which the mind and body must reach a harmonious balance, because the entire subsequent life depends on the quality of this first phase of development. • Education that is conceived as giving aid to life must always be in harmony with our pasts and look to the future. We have been inserted into the giant experiment of life called evolution, which has taken about 5 billion years. All of this history is reproduced in individual development; ontogenesis recapitulates phylogenesis. (Note: A 19th-century hypothesis that suggests the development of an individual organism [ontogeny] mirrors or repeats the evolutionary history of its species [phylogeny]. (Quattrocchi Montanaro, 2009, p. 6)

not passive recipients of their culture's knowledge; rather, they are active participants in their own learning, having an intrinsic drive to explore and master their environment (NRC & IOM, 2000). In practice, these early learning settings will include enriching experiences that allow for freedom of choice and movement, and extended opportunities to engage with all that is offered.

Just as notable are longitudinal evidence from epigenetic studies that warn of troubling impacts some experiences may have on children's development. For example, early hardships caused by generational poverty, violence in the home, or a primary caretaker who suffers from depression or addiction can serve as harmful stressors in a young child's life. These experiences, unfortunately, can have far-reaching impact on the health and well-being of individuals throughout their lives.

> [These] critical or sensitive periods provide unmatched opportunities for both positive and negative influences on developing biological systems. Above and beyond well-known impacts on early brain development, increasing evidence is also pointing to the importance of the prenatal period and first few years after birth for the development of core immune functions, metabolic regulation, and other physiological systems that can affect long-term wellbeing. Without dismissing the influence of adult lifestyle (including nutrition, exercise, and sleep) on physical health, early adversity can increase the risk for many of the most common chronic diseases that appear later in life and that incur substantial costs to society. (National Scientific Council on the Developing Child, 2020, p. 13)

It cannot be overstated—the foundational experiences offered to a young infant and toddler, including the quality of relationships and interactions with the adults who care for them, will have far-reaching influence on their development.

From the moment the child enters the world and takes their first breath outside their mother's body, they have begun their journey toward independence. Their caregivers take charge of their "sleep, feeding and emotional growth (that) become one of the priorities of parenthood and a key time for healthy mental and physical development and optimal health expectations" (Indrio et al., 2023, p. 2). In their first year, the child learns by watching, hearing, feeling, exploring, and interacting with the environment around them. Every environment is a learning environment. Whether in the home, the park, or an early care environment, infants have an unconscious capacity to take in information through their senses (Figure 3.1). Montessori (1967/1995) referred to this capacity as the child's "absorbent mind" (p. 266).

Though children in their first year of life may be referred to as prelinguistic—not yet able to verbally express their thoughts and feelings—they are in fact taking in any language they hear around them. Patricia Kuhl (2010) refers to infants as "linguistic geniuses" as they determine the sounds that are part of their language. According to Kuhl, before children reach their first birthday, regardless of what language is spoken to them or in which country they reside, linguistically they are "citizens of the world." Her research shows that infants have an incredible ability

Figure 3.1. An Infant, Alert and Absorbing the Environment

to discriminate the sounds of all languages. But after this first precious year, they become, like us, culture-bound listeners, able to distinguish only the sounds of the language (or languages, for those children fortunate to be learning two languages simultaneously) they hear most frequently. Though infants do not yet have verbal language, they demonstrate their linguistic recognition by communicating through other forms of expressions. Their smiles, cries, and coos communicate joy, hunger, engagement, and a host of other human experiences. They further engage you with their eyes and their leg and arm movements. Their intense survey of your face means they want to continue this "conversation"—and when they turn their gaze away, they demonstrate they are ready for a break.

Physical development is also a miraculous span of growth as children move from lying down to rolling over and sitting up, crawling, pulling up, standing, and sometimes even walking within their first year. As they become toddlers, once the basic movements are automatic, they acquire more intricate and extended movements like running, opening a drawer, wiping a face, and tiptoeing. Montessori (2007), makes visible small moments that demonstrate children's growth and development through her own observations of children:

> He [the baby] is developing his muscles. If you watch him closely, you may see perhaps the little fingers open one by one instead of all together—that is a great progress. Gradually he is becoming master of his own fingers, he chuckles with joy as he drops the rattle and you patiently pick it up for him. There is no naughtiness in him, he has no need of external discipline, soon he will drop this occupation of his own accord and perhaps his little toes will become for him next the most interesting things in the world. (p. 26)

Montessori noted that even the youngest children contribute to their own development and demonstrate independence as they actively explore their environment, make choices based on their individual interests, respond to caregivers through their behavior, and actively construct their understanding of the world through the many interactions they have with the people, materials, and experiences made available to them.

ENVIRONMENTAL RESPONSE TO DEVELOPMENTAL NEEDS (0–3)

The early weeks of a newborn's life are a precious opportunity for a family to welcome and bond with their new child. When very young children are also cared for outside the home, this presents another opportunity when they can be nurtured within a well-designed environment adapted to meet their individual development. Of the more than 4,500 independent Montessori schools in the United States (AMS, 2025), many offer infant and toddler environments that fulfill the youngest children's needs quite well.

"Montessori was one of the first researchers who shone a new light on how to view newborns; that is, they are individuals who are separate from their mothers and yet, inextricably tied to them, requiring special and delicate attention" (Honegger, 2023, p. 130). Like all environments designed for children, they begin with trained adults who focus on safety and opportunities for individualized development. An observer entering the space will note that the environment is peaceful though active. It is clean and unobstructed from unnecessary items—everything has a purpose. The space and the arrangement of all it contains promotes a sense of calm and safety to the infant. For the observer, the child-sized furniture may make the room feel bottom-heavy, which is to ensure children are able to do things for themselves. The furniture supports a child's balance, their early steps, and their independence while they sit to eat lunch. What an observer may not see are playpens or walkers or high chairs—the types of furniture that contains a child rather than supports their developmental need for movement.

The shelves contain developmentally appropriate materials that are attractively arranged and easily accessible to the children. The shelves and tables are low, and there are many places near the floor for children to be. There are mirrors so they may examine their reflections while reclined on a soft cushion, boxes and trays with simple items to explore, and even the art is hung mere inches from the floor for children to enjoy! The entirety of the Montessori environment stimulates the senses, serving as an invitation to explore. It's very design calls to children with the purpose of helping them meet their full potential:

> Although the desire to learn, grow, and "become" is inherent in the biology of early childhood, it is also a characteristic that is open to modification based on individual experience. When the environment supports a child's emerging sense of agency (i.e., the feeling of being able to influence events and thus having an impact on one's life), his

> or her motivation to act on the world flourishes. When experience fails to support (or punishes) such action, a child's motivation diminishes, shifts, or finds problematic outlets. Early environments that facilitate competence and a sense of personal efficacy are more likely to foster children who do well. When opportunities for agency are limited, psychological growth is more likely to be compromised. (NRC & IOM, 2000, p. 32)

In Montessori 0–3 environments, materials support children's development. Materials are available, accessible, and children experience agency as they select activities in their environment as their interests guide them. Children lead the structure of the day, when they eat, when they sleep, when they are ready to engage with others. And with the support of responsive caretakers who build nourishing relationships, infants and toddlers flourish.

HOW THE 0–3 MONTESSORI CLASSROOM SUPPORTS PHYSICAL DEVELOPMENT

The Infant (Nido) Community

The infant environment begins with meeting basic needs like sleeping, eating, and initial explorations of touch, sight, and sound. Though shelving and materials appear Lilliputian to the observer, the intentional design will meet the ever-changing physical development needs of young children as they progress from lying down to sitting up, crawling, and becoming early walkers. Soft cushioned blankets and mats allow children to lie down comfortably. Whether the child is in a prone or supine position, there are interesting items available for the child to consume through their senses. There are comfortable spots with mats, allowing infants to gaze at mobiles, to watch their own movements in a mirror, and to reach for nearby toys. Their hands, arms, and legs being unrestrained allows for a host of movements that will grow more purposeful over the coming months (Figure 3.2).

Infants' senses take in information from their environment even prior to birth. They grew accustomed to voices they heard and reacted to bright light while in utero. Now all of their senses are primed to take in all that is available to them in this new physical environment, ready for careful stimulation. What better way to feed them than with visuals of all that nature offers outside their window: the blue sky, blooming plants, rustling tree leaves, and rays of sunshine dancing along a nearby window prism. More fully experiencing the room from the child's perspective may require the observer to move to the floor to recognize the many treasures available to them!

The Montessori environment is carefully arranged and minimalistic—everything has a purpose. There are cubbies for tucking away belongings, a mat with a mirror for the child to see themselves as they move, a kiosk with bars in front of a mirror on the wall so the child can watch as they pull themself up, and chairs both weaning and slatted—the first with extra support and the second for easy moving.

Figure 3.2. An Infant Purposefully Reaching for a Suspended Ring

There are tables, foot-stools, benches, shelves, floor beds, and cupboards. All but a few items serve the adult serving the child, such as the changing table and rocking chair.

In an infant environment, the materials are what Dr. Montessori described as aids to development (see Table 3.2). A good example of what might be considered an aid is a type of manipulative, such as a small cylinder that contains a bell. It's offered when the child is not yet crawling but is able to spend time on their belly. The cylinder is colorful and at first seems like a rattle—which it can be—but it also encourages the child to hold their head upright for extended periods of time, increasing their dexterity as they reach for and grasp items, even supporting core strength and the determination to reach. Reaching promotes slithering movement—a stage prior to crawling and a milestone infants work toward achieving.

Clothing must be comfortable and practical. Routines established by caregivers offer stability to a new human as they begin to explore their world. A child's needs are simple. Sleep, food, and play/engagement are the essential elements of their daily routine, and they should be offered in that order, over and over throughout the day.

Table 3.2. Aids to Development in the Infant (Nido) Community

In the infant community, the areas of the curriculum are grouped in support of particular skill acquisition and are named in a literal way.

The Aids to Visual and Auditory Stimulation—These are mobiles, plants, pictures, art, and music. The child can be at any stage of gross motor to participate with these aids although the mobiles are generally for the child as they lie on their back.

The Aids to Visual, Auditory, and Tactile Stimulation are things like a bell or ring on a ribbon, a ball to kick, beads for grasping, interlocking disks or rings, a rubber ball with protrusions, a sphere with little balls, teething objects, and rattles. These aids are generally for children who cannot sit up on their own and interact with their hands, mouth, and eyes to learn.

The Aids to Eye-Hand Coordination include a punch ball; a basket of familiar objects; an ovoid, sphere, or cube in a container; a box with a ball and tray or a box with a ball and drawer; a box with balls to push; or a box with knitted balls. These are for children who can sit to engage with things.

The Aids for Crawling, Pulling, Standing, and Walking include balls, an orb with a ball, a cylinder with a bell, knitted or cloth balls, a heavy stool, the bar, and a push wagon or spin top. As described, these items roll away or are strong and supportive for the moving child.

Aids to Development of Equilibrium and Eye-Hand Coordination are rings on a rocking base, spindles with napkin rings, rings on a stable base, locks and keys, household objects, and a basket with rings and pegs. They support more intricate handwork in the child who is moving or on the way to being ambulatory.

If local licensing permits, Montessori infant rooms may offer floor beds instead of cribs for children to sleep on. Once they can roll and crawl, the transition from sleeping to waking can then be determined by the child alone without dependence on an adult. When children wake from a floor bed instead of a crib, they learn to explore their environment on their own as they naturally wake up. There's seldom crying or calling for an adult. Instead the room design has been carefully prepared, it is safe and clean, with developmentally appropriate activities prepared and available for the child to explore on the floor themselves.

Freedom is a term often related to Montessori classrooms. In practice, daily schedules include uninterrupted time for children to engage in the environment along with agency to choose which materials they will use—hallmark features of a Montessori environment beginning with the youngest children. There are materials to encourage infants' movement as they grasp items with their whole hand, explore textures, pinch fabric, play with balls, or investigate any of the above with their eyes and mouth. Through the progression of children's physical development, from holding their head up, to turning over, to sitting up with support, the materials offered to the child are all to further their development and prepare them for later experiences awaiting them in the toddler classroom.

The Toddler Community

Children who are moving on their feet with ease demonstrate readiness for the Toddler classroom. Typically, the Toddler room will be the most appropriate environment for children between 12 and 14 months and 2 and a half or 3 years of age. At 12 to 14 months, children learn to sit, crawl, walk, and explore. They will gain more confidence as they do things for themselves, use vocabulary and language, and refine the fine and gross motor skills necessary to function independently.

As in all Montessori environments, this space contains child-sized furniture, Montessori materials to support skill acquisition, elements of nature, books, and tools necessary to accomplish tasks. It contains both aids and activities for the children to use to further their development. Though children at this age are not yet offered formal lessons, they are instead connected to the learning materials through an adult offering and modeling their use (see Table 3.3). Due to the developmental focus of movement and independence, even the furniture is a developmental material in the toddler classroom. Children are encouraged to move chairs and small floor tables as needed.

Montessori recognized children's deep desire or internal drive in key areas of their development—a drive for independence, for movement, and for agency. She used the term *normalized* to define a peaceful state of equilibrium that children achieve when the "physical and mental energies of the body are integrated, work together. With this integration, the child progresses along her unique path of development . . . (by a) vital urge that pushes living organisms to achieve their unique developmental potential" (Orion, 2009, p. 79). However, she warned that certain experiences could shift a child away from their typical path of development. As an example, when an environment inhibits the child's ability to move, there can be many ramifications, or what Montessori referred to as deviations in the child. Judith Orion (2009) points out that

> All children learn to move easily, effortlessly, but they need a great deal of practice in achieving this ability. When we put them into containers, when we constantly ask/request/demand them to stop moving and be still, we are inhibiting this urge. We are causing this split between the physical and mental energies of the body. Deviations will occur. (p. 80)

Consider the time adults spend encouraging children to take their first steps, cheering them on as they move across the span of a living room couch and eventually the very room itself! These opportunities nurture their desire for physical movement. The child is content as their inner drive for movement is supported. However, almost as soon as they've mastered movement, many toddler environments become outfitted with high chairs and pack-'n-plays or other collapsible enclosures aimed to keep children safe but that also contain and restrain them. Young toddlers do not need extended "circle time" or reminders to sit "criss-cross

Table 3.3. Aids to Development in the Toddler Classroom

Materials for the Refinement of Hand Movements are activities like spooning, pouring, pouring through a funnel, sewing, gluing, the use of scissors, and folding. These Practical Life exercises are suited for a child who sits on a chair at a table.

Aids to the Development of the Stereognostic Sense. These exercises are simply items in a bag that can be discerned by the hand and mind of the child. They start with the most common and gradually get more difficult to decipher. This is the first introduction to using the stereognostic sense of knowing something that you cannot see.

Language Exercises include common objects of many kinds, objects with matching cards, picture cards on their own, books, rhythmic language, self-expression, and the questioning exercise, which draws answers out of a child and gives practice in verbal expression.

Music and Movement brings musical instruments, singing, dancing, and games.

Art includes scribbling, an easel with chalk of tempura paints, and clay.

Practical Life Exercises

Food is an important area of the curriculum and introduces preparing food, setting the table, serving the food, eating, cleaning up, washing dishes, and drying dishes.

Care of the Person Activities involves undressing, dressing, storage of clothing, handwashing, handwashing in the sink, brushing hair, wiping the nose, cleaning shoes, brushing teeth, and dressing frames, which are wooden frames with simple buttons, hooks, and Velcro for practice with opening and closing garments and footwear.

Care of the Indoors includes wiping a table, washing a table with soap, dusting, sweeping, mopping cleaning glass, polishing a mirror, polishing wood, dusting plants, watering plants, flower arranging, washing cloths, and hanging up cloths to dry. All of these require the child to be stable on their feet and walking.

Care of the Outdoors involves activities like germinating seeds, raking leaves, planting a garden, watering plants, weeding a garden, and sweeping. Again, these are introduced to a walking child.

Grace and Courtesy lessons are not spelled out specifically, but include how to respond when someone falls by offering a hand or asking if they are okay. The adult models these reactions for all students, and they become a strong element in curating the kind culture in the classroom.

Movement of Furniture provides opportunities for the toddlers to carry a chair, sit on a chair, carry a table, carry a stool, carry a bench, and use a rug.

applesauce." Rather, they require incalculable opportunities for movement to build independence and gross and fine motor skills.

An observer in the Toddler room will be intrigued and inspired by the busyness of these children. They are so engaged—trying and working and moving and interacting. They are so capable, you cannot help but be impressed by their abilities and independence as you watch. For toddlers, the moving of furniture work in the toddler curriculum is the culmination of all movements together for the

Figure 3.3. A Toddler, Washing Hands at the Sink

child beginning at approximately 20 months. The child must put it all together—steadiness on their feet, the specific hold on the item, and transporting it to another place with equilibrium and awareness of the rest of the room. This is not to mention the confidence that will feed the next wave of development. Older toddlers will demonstrate even more purpose in their movement, such as washing their hands, helping to sort freshly washed towels, or laying out plates and utensils for lunch (Figure 3.3). These are shared tasks that support the child's internal need for purposeful engagement that in turn supports their physical development. As Montessori noted, "Children love to do these things [Practical Life activities] for themselves and they learn to be careful and precise in their movements. This is both education **of** movement, because there is refinement of muscular co-ordination when the work is carefully done, and education **through** movement, because these activities involve judgement and will, self-discipline, and an appreciation of orderliness" (2007, p. 49).

Studies point to the positive relationship between children's motor development, cognitive development, and later school readiness skills. As they experience progress in one domain there is often a connection to progress in another domain (National Academies of Sciences, Engineering, and Medicine, 2015).

HOW THE 0–3 MONTESSORI CLASSROOM SUPPORTS COGNITIVE DEVELOPMENT

A child is born with billions of neurons, but most are not yet connected (ZERO TO THREE, n.d.). The strength or weakness of a child's brain architecture is greatly dependent on their daily experiences that in turn will support all future learning. In these early years, neural pathways are formed, leading to new sensory pathways like vision and hearing, leading in turn to language skills and higher cognitive functions (National Scientific Council on the Developing Child, 2020, 2023). Each of these early pathways are part of an integrated and reciprocal system of children's development. One skill can in turn lead to the development of multiple skills.

> Changes in one domain often impact other areas and highlight each area's importance. For example, as children begin to crawl or walk, they gain new possibilities for exploring the world. This mobility in turn affects both their cognitive development and their ability to satisfy their curiosity, underscoring the importance of adaptations for children with disabilities that limit their mobility. Likewise, language development influences a child's ability to participate in social interaction with adults and other children; such interactions, in turn, support further language development as well as further social, emotional, and cognitive development. (National Association for the Education of Young Children, 2020, p. 9)

Providing an environment for children that is rich in language, purposeful activities, and connections with nature is a powerful way to meet their cognitive needs. In the Nido vignette at the beginning of our chapter, the language element is evident as the adults read books as often as they can. Books and stories are intentionally selected, animals do not talk, nor are magic spells offered to make a character feel better. To support their cognitive development so that they may better know who they are and what is available to them in the world, caregivers focus on what is visible and tangible to the child. They describe attributes of living and non-living things, noting aloud an object's color, shape, texture, function, or use. They use descriptive language to explain or reason why an action occurred. "You rolled the ball across the table and it fell to the floor! Shall we do that again?" (Dean & LeMoine, 2019). These new humans need to know what is real in their world and a foundation of trust is established by offering the truth in the world to them. This approach also builds children's background knowledge and vocabulary, avoids potential confusion in future learning, and provides a model for honesty between the adult and the child.

One evidence-based approach to building children's vocabulary and concept development is through a strategy identified as Serve and Return (Center for the Developing Child, n.d.). As with all learning and development, it builds on the safe and nurturing relationship between the infant or toddler and their caregiver. The approach works through shared attention, as the adult takes the cue from the child to build a narrative that reflects what is of interest to the child. For example, if an infant gazes at a mobile dancing above their head, the caregiver may say aloud to the child, "Do you see those shapes above you? I see a red square. And there's a blue circle." The important element is that the adult takes their cue from the child. When the infant glances away from the mobile, it might be a sign to pause, giving the child a chance to enjoy the mobile visually. Later, as children are able to express their responses verbally, the interaction will be a bit different. The adult will still lead with what is of interest to the child, but will also provide ample time to hear the child's response and create an intentional shared dialogue. In practice it may look like this:

Adult: "You've been watching the betta fish in the tank this morning. What did you notice?"
Toddler: "The fish swim. The fish eat."
Adult: "He ate his food? He must have been hungry."
Toddler: "I hungry too."
Adult: "You are hungry? What did you have for breakfast this morning?"
Toddler: "I ate pancakes!" (Child's attention returns to the betta fish)
Adult: "Did you notice his long fin at the top? I think we have a book that describes the betta fish. Do you want to read that together after you've finished observing the fish in the tank?"

In this example, the adult prompted a conversation based on what was of interest to the child. Grammatical errors were not brought to the child's attention ("eat vs. ate"); instead, the adult simply modeled the correct language. There are five easy steps that can be used in everyday moments in the home or classroom (Table 3.4). The caregiver can make connections and label what a child is interested in, an emotion they may be experiencing, or an object the child may be reaching for—all of these opportunities will help to develop early language skills long before a child utters their first words aloud.

As J. Ronald Lally (2009) pointed out, the most critical curriculum components at this stage of development are not lessons or lesson plans, but rather the planning of settings and experiences that allow learning to take place.

HOW THE 0–3 MONTESSORI CLASSROOM SUPPORTS CHARACTER DEVELOPMENT—PURPOSE AND SOCIAL INTELLIGENCE

> We see the child who is freely active change in character. Movement is correlated with character—just with intelligence, but also with character.
>
> —Maria Montessori, 1946, p. 160

Purpose and social intelligence are two of the character traits nurtured in the 0–3 classroom. Purpose, the commitment to making a meaningful contribution

Table 3.4. Five Steps to "Serve and Return" to Build Language Skills

1. Notice the serve and share the child's focus of attention.

   Is the child looking or pointing at something? Making a sound or facial expression? Moving those little arms and legs? That's a serve. The key is to pay attention to what the child is focused on.

2. Return the serve by supporting and encouraging.

   You can offer children comfort with gentle words, support them, play with them. You can acknowledge them by making a sound or facial expression. Smiling and nodding will let a child know you're noticing the same thing. Or you can pick up an object a child is pointing to and bring it closer.

3. Give it a name!

   When you return a serve by naming what a child is seeing, doing, or feeling, you make important language connections in their brain, even before the child can talk or understand your words. You can name anything—a person, a thing, an action, a feeling, or a combination.

4. Take turns . . . and wait. Keep the interaction going back and forth.

   Every time you return a serve, give the child a chance to respond. Taking turns can be quick (from the child to you and back again) or go on for many turns. **Waiting is crucial.** Children need time to form their responses, especially when they're learning so many things at once. Waiting helps keep the turns going.

5. Practice endings and beginnings.

   Children signal when they're done or ready to move on to a new activity. They might let go of a toy, pick up a new one, or turn to look at something else. Or they may walk away, start to fuss, or say, "All done!" When you share a child's focus, you'll notice when they're ready to end the activity and begin something new.

Adapted from The Center for the Developing Child (2017).

to the world, is foundational at every level of the Montessori classroom. Though this section addresses purpose in young children's development, it's important to note the many ways purpose is embedded in these early learning environments. Materials are purposely curated in the environment. Furniture selection is purposeful. Human interactions are purposeful. And the goal of these purposeful elements is the individualized development of the child.

According to Angela Duckworth, purpose is one's "commitment to making a meaningful contribution to the world . . . it gives you forward momentum . . . it motivates . . . (and) with a strong sense of purpose, you flourish" (Duckworth, n.d.-a). In a Montessori classroom, even the youngest children can find purpose in their work. Putting on shoes, washing hands, and watering a plant are all meaningful activities.

STUDENT REFLECTION

Trinity (attended) the toddler house. . . . I remember the sense of belonging, small community group, ability to explore and her love of books.

—Trinity, age 25, Montessori student 8 years

The Practical Life activities are simple and direct, using familiar objects and carried out with a goal in mind. It is amazing what a child can do if you give them the opportunity! Remember, for example, the girl in the vignette who peeled and sliced the egg to eat it in the Toddler classroom. This work is important because the child becomes aware of their labors. This builds confidence and autonomy, reasons why the process in these activities is even more important than the result. If toddlers want to help wash dishes after snack, it's the process that matters most. The product—clean dishes—though certainly important, can be managed by being placed in the dishwasher at the end of the day. These activities are the foundation of building a classroom community. And engaged, confident, independent children are likely to participate in lifelong learning endeavors.

Duckworth adds "awe" as an element of purpose. A child will experience awe in everyday moments that create a "feeling of encountering vast mysteries that we don't immediately understand" (Duckworth, n.d.-j). Think of that young boy, new to the toddler environment, as described in the second vignette. He experienced the awe of connecting the photo in his classroom with something he knew in real life. "It's snow!" he said with excitement. For the young infant, moments of mystery and novel experiences abound. An infant will experience awe as the branch of a tree sways in the breeze or when a rolling ball suddenly appears at the end of a ramp. These everyday moments engage a young child and sustain their attention, supporting their resilience to persevere and feel good about all they've accomplished that day.

Social intelligence, the ability to connect with other people, is another important consideration in character development. For infants and toddlers, relationships are paramount. Duckworth points to a holy trinity, or three essential elements, shared in healthy interpersonal relationships: "the first is understanding—seeing the other person for who they are . . . The second is validation—valuing the other person's perspective, even if it differs from your own. And third is caring—expressing authentic affection, warmth, and concern" (Duckworth, n.d.-i). This is the very foundation of learning and development in a Montessori classroom. We can see this in both vignettes at the beginning of this chapter. The adult in the Nido environment supports the transition from parent to child in a relaxed and caring way by holding the child for a moment before putting them down and waiting for their attention to switch to their classroom. In the Toddler classroom vignette, the adult acknowledges the new child's need for closeness and is available for comfort even while working with other children. The children are respected for who they are and what they bring to the classroom. Their perspectives are validated and authentic affection and warmth are demonstrated by their caregivers. The relationship is foundational to everything.

THE ROLE OF THE ADULT IN THE 0–3 CLASSROOM

As you enter a 0–3 Montessori environment, you'll note the pivotal role adults play in the classroom. You will hear a peaceful hum, possibly soothing background music, perhaps an ongoing adult narration of an infant's or a toddler's actions spoken in a soothing voice. The Association Montessori Internationale (AMI) requires caregivers working with infants and toddlers to have "(a)n understanding of the child's development [that] allows Montessori environments to meet the needs of the infant and foster a sense of belonging, independence, and language acquisition enabling children to feel able and capable" (n.d.-b)

The American Montessori Society's School Accreditation Standards (2023) require infant and toddler educators to facilitate a curriculum "based on 6 integrated developmental areas: sensory and perceptual, cognitive, physical, gross and fine motor, self-help skills, and social/emotional development. The learning environment fosters freedom of movement, integrates daily routines, and provides experiences that develop a child's growth and independence" (AMS Standard 3.3.1, p. 3).

To achieve these objectives, Montessori guides leading 0–3 environments are trained in all domains of children's development. Their professionalism mirrors expectations outlined in *ZERO TO THREE's Critical Competencies for Infant-Toddler Educators* (Dean et al., 2019):

- Adults value each child.
- They understand that children's growth and development is nurtured along a continuum.
- They design inclusive, positive, encouraging environments that reflect the unique strengths and needs of the children in their care.

Caregiving practice is grounded in relationships, the bridge to supporting children's development and learning.

> Children grow and thrive in the context of close and dependable relationships that provide love and nurturance, security, responsive interaction, and encouragement for exploration. Without at least one such relationship, development is disrupted and the consequences can be severe and long-lasting. (NRC & IOM, 2000, p. 7)

The importance of the adult and the quality of the relationship they develop with the young child is paramount.

These relationship-based principles founded in contemporary research (NRC & IOM, 2000; ZTT, 2019) were noted through early observations conducted by Adele Costa Gnocchi, a colleague of Dr. Montessori who led a study for the development of the 0–3 pedagogy in 1946. Gnocchi recognized that from the moment of birth, newborns demonstrated unique qualities and were active participants in their own development. She "paid special attention to the ways in which newborns react(ed) to changes—in people, places, and habits—and to changes in their caregivers' behaviors, how the caregivers handle(d) newborns" (Honegger, 2023, p. 130). She noted that infants thrived in particular contexts:

- when they experienced loving and reliable relationships with their caregivers,
- spent their days in environments with schedules that were intentionally predictable and peaceful, and
- when they received responsive and gentle care that was free of sudden movement, especially during bathing and dressing.

Later, Grazia Honegger Fresco, a student of Gnocchi, observed that infants were responsive to consistency in their environments, their caregivers, and their daily routines. For the youngest children, this need for consistency is nurtured through relational security, a form of attachment theory noted in the works of Magda Gerber, Emmi Pikler, and Mary Ainsworth. Gerber believed babies had "an essential need to be touched and held, but she also believed the positive effect of touch was greatly diminished when there was little direct attention paid to the baby. 'What is the value of being held or touched if it's only the skin that is in contact? What about your minds connecting, or to become more philosophical, your souls?'" (Lansbury, 2013). Both physical and emotional connections between the infant and their caregiver are foundational to all other development.

> The importance of this first bond cannot be emphasized enough, as it is fundamental to the child's subsequent development of independence . . . every child sees their own reflection in the eyes of the adult, and . . . special attention [should be given] to the moment that the child transitions from the mother's arms—the child's first environment—to the care of the nursery . . . that begins with the educator's welcoming gaze and is supported by an educational environment intentionally prepared for the newborn. (Honegger, 2023, p. 132)

With this secure attachment in place, the adult will also help facilitate children's interactions with peers by creating dyads and small groups. They prepare the children's environment with engaging play materials and remain close by to model appropriate behavior. When needed, they may also redirect children, as well as offer positive reinforcement (Dean et al., 2019).

The adult is also a facilitator of learning and development.

> Infant-toddler educators need to draw upon their knowledge of individual children's interests, temperaments, culture and language, and physical needs to ensure they are providing access to objects and experiences that challenge children's skills and understanding, while allowing for success that will reinforce children's desire to repeat such exploration in the future. (Dean et al., 2019, p. 42)

Some learning experiences might be spontaneous in reaction to events during the day, while others may be previously planned. For example, when a toddler shows interest in birds they've seen outside, the adult places a bird feeder in the window and makes laminated images of local birds and small picture books about birds available to support the child's learning.

The adult must be in the moment, watching and then modeling; for example, using language in a precise way, narrating an activity the child is engaged in, or using words to intentionally make connections between objects in the environment and their correct names. Long before a child utters their first word, they are absorbing the language heard from family members and caregivers. New concepts and vocabulary are explored through book reading. They learn through the back-and-forth exchanges they hear, through sign language they are introduced to, and through their own early attempts of expressive language.

The adult is conscious of the novelty of all that surrounds the child. Pregnant pauses will be necessary to allow time for the child to assimilate all the information their senses are taking in from their environment. Adults offer children space and time to notice something rather than pointing things out overtly. If children are deeply engaged in an activity, there will be ample time provided for them to complete their tasks. The adult keeps the big picture in mind—this is a growing and developing human and quite quickly, this wee child will need to be able to function independently. Wouldn't it be wonderful to do so and be self-satisfied, happy, and contribute to the world they are living in?

Adults are also self-aware. This begins with reflection of one's own culture, values, and beliefs so educators can lead with just and equitable practices with all children (ZERO TO THREE, 2023). They are also aware if they offer too much support they may be a barrier to the child's development.

The adult, always observant and reflective, asks themselves, what does the child need? And how can this environment provide what is needed? It's a delicate balance between being an active observer and offering assistance only when it is truly required for the child to successfully complete a task. Adults scaffold learning that's individualized to meet the needs of each child. And to lead this intricate work, educators are attentive, have keen observation skills, and possess a strong understanding of children's early development. If the child is not yet able to complete an entire task independently, the adult must consider what parts they are able to complete. Any activity can be broken down into smaller steps so children can participate and find meaning in their work. If they are not yet able to put their jacket on without support, could they remove it from their hook in the cubby? Could they lay the jacket on the floor with the collar at their feet? Next,

Figure 3.4. A Toddler Has Chosen an Activity From the Shelf of Aids in the Toddler Classroom

could they place their arms in each sleeve and lift the jacket over their head so it gentle slips onto their body? The adult's role is to model activities, such as care of self (washing hands, brushing hair) and care of the environment (placing books on a shelf, washing a table). In the infant room vignette, one adult modeled how to open various containers for the child. These authentic Practical Life exercises promote children's agency as they learn, in time, to be independent (Figure 3.4).

Adults who care for infants and toddlers are facilitators who guide each individual child in their quest toward their full potential. Each morning, before the children arrive, everything in the environment is made ready for the children. Everything in the classroom is of value to their development and can be an opportunity for a lesson. Each afternoon, before the classroom door is closed for the day, the adults review the children's progress and consider next steps for tomorrow based on today's work. They recognize the importance of consistency in their interactions and approaches. Their role is to support the child holistically—their physical, cognitive, and character development—recognizing that each child is unique and honoring individual variabilities in competencies and growth.

CHAPTER 4

Montessori 3–6 Classrooms

> . . . children construct their own characters, building up in themselves the qualities we admire. These do not spring from our example or admonishments, but they result solely from a long and slow sequence of activities carried out by the child himself between the ages of 3 and 6.
>
> —Montessori, 1967/1995, p. 259

A 3–6 Classroom Vignette

It was 8:45 on a Tuesday morning, and everyone was so busy already. A stool perched at the end of a Practical Life shelf offered a good view of the room in front and the snack and kitchen area behind. There was chatter and the opportunity to observe students engaged in various activities at many different levels—some on the floor, some at tables, and some standing, walking, and jumping! The movement sounds out of place in a classroom, but it was done with care around work on mats and it seemed a creative, joyful form of expression.

A lot of engagement was taking place in the snack-eating area. There were four occupied seats, with three boys happily chatting away. The fourth seemed to still be waking up or concentrating on nourishing his tiny body. In the other space, there was a mosaic of work mats displayed in different directions, some with long bead chains snaked around their surface. The mats also held wooden trays, and alongside part of the chain, tickets were laid out. The rest of the tickets were grouped together waiting to be placed. A small girl was working diligently on the sixth chain, a math material made of bars of six beads for counting out the multiples. The tickets hold the number of the last bead in the bar—for example, 6, 12, 18, and so on. She concentrated as she counted, named, retrieved, and placed the appropriate ticket at the end of each bead bar in the chain. She had an air of experience about her.

Two adults were in the room. Both spoke to the children in low, respectful tones, and their roles were very obvious. The guide was connecting children to materials, giving lessons to individuals or small groups all over the classroom. The assistant was supporting children in their work by answering questions or directing them to resources. It was a busy, joyful classroom, and the children were each engaged at different levels of skill and independence.

Beside the child with the long six chain (a chain of six bars connected with accompanying tickets showing the last number of each bar) was a mat with the long seven chain and all the number tickets showing the multiples of 7 up until 343 (7×7×7). A child around 5 years old was counting and placing the tickets on the last bead of each bead bar. He was focused and appeared experienced as well, but was not as confident in his work. He was counting very carefully—toward the last third of the chain—then turned his attention to the tickets to identify the correct number. He went back and counted the last bead bar again and searched again. He then made sure his unplaced tickets were all facing the right direction and went through them one by one looking for the number. He paused and looked around the classroom as if contemplating something. Then he got up and stood by the assistant while she spoke to another child. After a minute, he had a change of heart, went back and counted, searched again, and then paused. He spent some time looking at the whole chain, thinking. He saw a boy nearby looking on at his work and said, "I can't seem to find 238." The boy looked at the tickets, didn't see it, and shrugged. The first boy went back and counted. "238."

In the meantime, the child working on the six chain completed the activity, sharing her update with a big smile on her face with the classroom assistant, who asked, "Can you find the 216?" The girl quickly smiled and pointed to the last ticket on the last bead of the last bar. It was a quick formative assessment to determine if the child understood her work. The assistant smiled right back and took a photo of the girl with her work. The girl began to methodically put the work away—first the tickets, then the box, then the chain, then rolled up the rug and returned it to its home in the wooden bin standing on its end.

The other child who was working on the seven chain had reevaluated his options, and, catching the attention of the assistant, finally said, "I can't find the 238." The adult came over to the rug and commented on the tickets being so nicely organized. Then she straightened the tray and lo and behold, out popped the ticket. They looked at each other in amazement. The boy smiled and placed it quickly, as the adult disappeared. The boy took a much-needed recovery break for snack but returned after 5 minutes. He then counted and placed and finished all the way to 343 in no time. He looked over his work for a moment and then jumped right into putting it away.

THE CHILD IN THE 3–6 CLASSROOM

What an incredibly vibrant period of growth in children's development! As the child moves beyond toddlerhood, there is now a radical shift in what can be accomplished between the ages of 3 and 6 years old. As discussed in Chapter 3, activities offered in the toddler environment were fleeting and wholly dependent on children's sporadic interests or needs in a given moment. The adult served as the connector between the environment and the child's interests. In that introductory developmental space, children's movements were unconsciously navigated by a powerful internal compass.

Now as they enter the 3–6 classroom, children

> rapidly develop foundational capabilities on which subsequent development builds. In addition to their remarkable linguistic and cognitive gains, they exhibit dramatic progress in their emotional, social, regulatory, and moral capacities. All of these critical dimensions of early development are intertwined, and each requires focused attention. (NRC & IOM, 2000, p. 5)

Recent advances in neurobiology have generated a deeper appreciation of the many experiences and environmental influences on children's learning and development, again echoing Montessori's early observations. In *A New Vision for High-Quality Preschool Curriculum* (National Academies of Sciences, Engineering, and Medicine, 2024), the authors noted:

> The neurobiology of learning and the powerful influences of the early learning environment on brain development are central considerations in planning effective preschool curriculum. The principle that there are *sensitive periods* during early childhood when the capacity for learning is enhanced has been well established in specific domains (language, visual) and is the focus of ongoing investigation in cognitive, social, and emotional domains (Werker & Hensch, 2020; Woodard & Pollack, 2020). Broadly, *the existence of sensitive periods and related high neuroplasticity during the early years of life represent a window of opportunity for enhancing early learning, as specific skills and abilities are known to be absorbed or learned more readily during these periods.* In turn, because learning is a cumulative process, enhanced early learning can lead to long-term learning benefits. In contrast, when opportunities for environmental stimulation and expected experiential inputs are missed, the early years can be a period of unique vulnerability and can lead to learning challenges at later developmental periods. (p. 56, emphasis added)

STUDENT REFLECTION

I remember several materials like the metal insets, bead frame, letters on the floor. Most of my memories associated with materials are based on nostalgia seeing pictures of them or one-on-one lessons with my guides in the children's house. I loved the Practical Life shelf, which may well be why I'm coordinated now.

—Sarah, 20, Montessori student for 12 years

Figure 4.1. A 5-Year-Old Mentoring a 3-Year-Old to Construct the Pink Tower

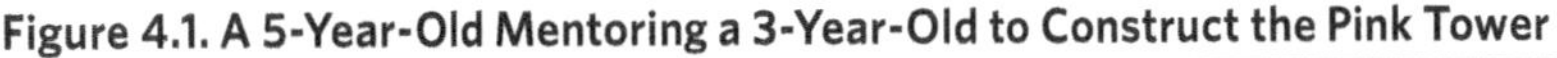

Children at this stage of development have a growing sense of self-awareness and demonstrate independence as part of their character development. They often prefer to complete tasks without assistance but are also happy to work alongside a peer, as displayed in the above vignette. Children whose independence was supported at the toddler stage will depend on adults less as they grow into the primary classroom. This is a good thing! Decision-making and doing things for themselves brings a great sense of accomplishment and joy. In the 3–6 classroom, children demonstrate a greater capacity for concentration, motivation, and agency. Morning work periods can extend up to 2 and a half to 3 hours each day. In our fast-paced world, where entertainment and information are mostly consumed in brief clips, the Montessori classroom offers space and time for children to return to materials multiple times to master content at their own pace. Children demonstrate a growing capacity to experience compassion for others, as well as understand social norms anticipated in different settings. Burgeoning relationships with peers lead them to navigate new interactions (Figure 4.1), to work collaboratively, to problem-solve, and to demonstrate leadership, as well as seek help from others when needed (CASEL, n.d.).

Though they're often referred to as "soft skills," research shows that these social qualities are predictive of children's adaptation to school and later academic success (California Department of Education, 2008).

ENVIRONMENTAL RESPONSE TO DEVELOPMENTAL NEEDS

During this incredible period of development, the Montessori primary classroom is intentionally designed to meet a wide range of needs and interests. It requires observant adults who command an acute attention to detail, and who care and trust in children's capabilities. The prepared environment influences human development and is responsive to the physical, cognitive, and character-building needs of young children.

> It is the child acting upon the environment that makes things happen. It is not the action of the teacher or the scope of the program for the child to learn. It is the child who creates his own activity through free selection of the materials. We don't teach; we present activities and give lessons that will appeal to the child's intelligence and natural curiosity; it is the child's inner teacher that does the rest. (Borbolla, 2020, p. 92)

Student Reflection

When I was 4, I remember using clay and water to make different land formations. I remember making booklets about birds. In elementary I remember using a bucket, rope, and water to learn about force. I remember getting to choose my own schedule and decide whether or not I wanted to go to recess or stay inside and finish work. I also remember having large cushions that we could make into a fort if we needed some silence or if we wanted a nice place to read.

—Sierra, 29, Montessori student for 7 years

An observer entering a primary classroom may first notice the child-sized shelves displaying multiple trays with organized learning materials, all easily accessible to learners. Upon closer inspection, the entire classroom is organized by learning domains to orient children. These materials, along with the design of the physical space of the classroom, and the interactions with the teacher and their peers, are the living "curriculum" that supports children's learning and development. Unlike the multitude of commercially available math, science, literacy, and social-emotional separately boxed curricula used in conventional early childhood settings, the Montessori classroom has an array of materials that span a 3-year comprehensive and integrated curriculum displayed and readily available for children's use.

Wherever a Montessori 3–6 classroom is situated in the world, there are shared observable aspects of the environment, "reflection(s) of beauty, truth and goodness" (Scocchera, 2002, as cited in Trabalzini, 2011, p. xi). Whether you're in a one-room Montessori learning pod in rural Iowa, a publicly funded Montessori elementary charter school in urban Cambridge, Massachusetts, or a university-based professional development model Montessori classroom located in Beijing, China, Montessori classrooms have a distinguishable universal design. For example, school accreditation standards set by the American Montessori Society (2023), require primary classrooms to "integrate the core areas of Practical Life, Sensorial, Math, and Language, as well as the Cultural Subjects" (AMS Standard 3.3.2). The following offers a brief look at each of these areas of the curriculum that live within the classroom environment.

STUDENT REFLECTION

The classrooms were great. They did well with mixing fun and learning while being supportive of me.

—Joshua, 26, Montessori student for 5 years

As Uma Ramani (2023) writes in her description of the Montessori 3–6 classroom, Practical Life exercises are irresistible to children, as "they want to participate in the care of the environment, the care of their person, and the social interactions that they have been observing from birth. The movements and the order intrinsic to each activity appeal to the [child's] sensitive periods . . . leading to functional independence" (p. 140). Materials on the shelf may include an assortment of trays, each containing a single exercise, such as pouring or scooping materials from one container to another. There are dressing frames, small wooden frames with different means of opening and closing attached colored fabric using buttons, snaps, zippers, and so on. Children can scrub tables, wash cups and dishes used during snack, water plants, and feed the fish in a small classroom aquarium—all exercises that reflect authentic daily living activities.

STUDENT REFLECTION

I think often of my experience washing my own snack dishes in my Montessori classroom as a child. I set up transferring trays for my current students as I recall how much I loved moving materials (colored water, rice, beads) from one container to another—pitchers, little bows with golden scoops . . . I also recall doing advanced math with the beads and playing banks and stores, and I think that helped form my ideas about the incredible thinking very young children are capable of.

—Sarae, age 49, Montessori student for 3 years

Materials in the Sensorial area support children's sensory perceptions, giving "form to the abstract qualities of matter such as color, shape, dimension, pitch, volume, texture, weight, and smell" (Ramani, 2023, p. 141). Materials include boxes of colored tablets to visually match by color or to organize by hue. Wooden cylinder blocks contain knobbed cylinders that vary by height, length, or width. The challenge is to find which cylinder fits in each hole in the block. There are materials to refine children's auditory skills, such as sound cylinders that include a set of 3 pairs of cylinders. Each pair contains sand, pebbles, or small bells that the child must pair solely through careful listening. These sensorial activities, among others, "offer the child the keys to the world, helping them classify, categorize, and find patterns in their environment" (Ramani, 2023, p. 142).

To expand on these experiences, the Montessori Math materials introduce children to

> concepts of number, counting, and calculation. Materials and activities are organized in the following groups: numbers one to ten, the decimal system, calculation, number syntax beyond ten, mental arithmetic, and fractions. In each group, concepts are introduced following the principle of isolation of difficulty, using concrete materials. Numbers are then associated with the concrete materials and finally, the child works only with numbers. (Ramani, 2023, p. 143)

These foundational exercises are introduced through the Number Rods, Spindle Boxes, the Teen and Ten Boards, and the Golden Bead materials (see Table 4.1). Lessons are structured, explicitly demonstrated, and as with all materials in the classroom, children are free to revisit the activities as often as needed to acquire mastery. In the 3–6 classroom, it is not unusual to see some children working on lessons focused on early numeracy (linear counting from 1 to 10), while others in the same classroom are adding and subtracting 4-digit numbers.

The Language materials offer "sound games (to) explore sounds in known words and lay the foundation of phonemic awareness. The letters of the alphabet are offered as symbols for the sounds of spoken language in the form of Sandpaper Letters that invite children to trace the letter as they look at the shapes and say the sound" (Ramani, 2023, p. 142). There are many 3-part cards consisting of 2 matching picture cards and a label (Table 4.1). Typically, the youngest children will match picture cards and older students will match both images and labels. Even before a child has developed the fine motor ability to write, they can use these card sets to put sounds together as they begin to understand the magic of language.

The Cultural materials introduce children "to the world of plants, animals, people, music, art, and literature" (Ramani, 2023, p. 144), initially related to those found in their own community, as well as expanding children's understanding of other places across the globe. Through stories, picture cards, and puzzle maps, children learn about the experiences of other children—the homes and communities they live in, the food they eat, and the clothes they wear. Through these materials, children learn "that they are a part of an interdependent whole that includes the Earth, plants, animals, and people around the globe and that they have a role to play in the harmony of this interdependent whole" (Ramani, 2023, p. 144).

The classroom includes child-sized tables and chairs that encourage children to work singly or in small groups. Small work mats also offer children dedicated floor space to conduct their work. As "too many materials in a classroom can be over-stimulating and can impede concentration" (Stephenson, 2012, p. 245), shelves and the materials they house are carefully curated. There is a hum of activity as children have the freedom to self-select work or to engage in individualized

Table 4.1. Sample of Montessori Materials

Number Rods 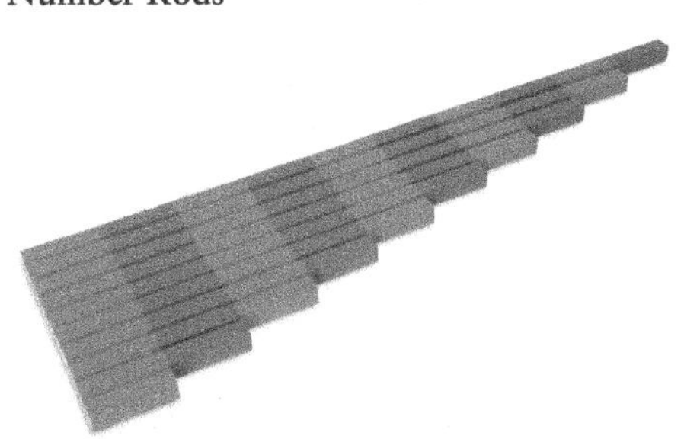	Introduces quantity 1–10 and their corresponding number names using length. Develops concepts in sequence and arithmetic.
Spindle Boxes 	Provides practice in associating quantity and symbol for numbers 0–9. Particular attention is given to the number 0.
Teen Board 	Explores numbers 11–19. Develops concepts in sequence and number combinations. Exercises are accompanied by bead bars.
Tens Board 	Explores the number names of the tens and the sequence of numbers 11–99. Exercises use bead bars.

(continued)

Table 4.1. (*continued*)

Golden Bead Materials 	Introduces the decimal system with concrete representations of numbers. Includes various components for addition, subtraction, multiplication, and division.
3-Part Cards—Land and Water Forms 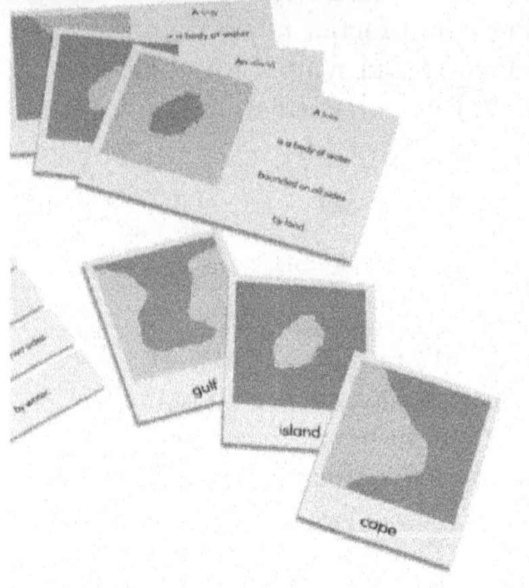 	Six sets of Land and Water Forms cards for matching exercises.
Dressing Frame—Buttons 	Develops hand-eye coordination and independence by teaching children to button large buttons with focused motor skill practice.

lessons alongside a teacher or a small group of peers. "The Montessori environment is filled with motion: children select materials, someone sweeps the floor, another waters the flowers. The children are concentrating on their tasks, which fulfill a specific meaning. The environment requires them to know how to move calmly and with poise" (Ahlquist, 2023, p. 121). Children's interactions go beyond mere use of instructional materials; rather, the child is caring for the classroom environment—a component of Practical Life in the Montessori classroom.

HOW THE 3-6 MONTESSORI CLASSROOM SUPPORTS PHYSICAL DEVELOPMENT

> From the moment of birth, the child takes in the Practical Life of his environment and makes it the foundation of his personality. Through the work of the absorbent mind, the child incarnates his environment and the behavior patterns and values of the community into which he is born. On the basis of this he lays the foundation of his intellect, his will, his movements. Impelled by his need to be part of the human narrative, the newborn begins to act on his environment. In the process, the intellect, the will, and the movements get strengthened and refined and the child develops as an individual. Intelligence and character develop through the use of the hands. The activities of Practical Life become the means for the creation and development of the self.
>
> —Ramani, 2013, p. 51

All interactions within the classroom environment at this age involve movement—effortful fine and gross motor movement! Montessori said that "the inclusion of movement in everything a child does is essential in the primary classroom. It is through movement that one learns to express oneself" (1967/1995, p. 172). This is why opportunities for movement are built into the classroom's very functioning. For example, there is a need for a mat when children work on the floor. The mat provides a boundary for work and visually organizes the child. Floor mats are retrieved from a basket on one side of the room and then unrolled for use. Some rugs scale almost the height of the child's shoulder. The child retrieves a mat before selecting their floor work and unrolls it in preparation for the activity. When finished with their work, the child returns materials to the shelf and then rolls their mat back up and returns it to the tall basket where the mats reside. To encourage movement, activities such as the bead chains, described in the vignette, are moved from the cabinet to the floor mat. Once they have completed the lesson, students are responsible for returning the bead chain to the cabinet, along with the small boxes that hold the number tickets, and for rolling up their mat and returning it to its rightful place ready for the next person—only then is the activity complete. This is an age for movement, not passive listening.

Science journalist Annie Murphy Paul (2021) wrote about the difference in learning when new information is learned through reading or listening to lectures versus learning that occurs when we're engaged both mentally and physically:

> When we're charged with learning and remembering new material our tendency is to lean heavily on visual and auditory modes: reading it over, saying it aloud. This

> approach has its limits; in particular, research demonstrates that our memory for what we have heard is remarkably weak. Our memory for what we have done, however—for physical actions we have undertaken—is much more robust. Linking movement to the material to be recalled creates a richer and therefore more indelible "memory trace" in the brain. In addition, movements engage a process called procedural memory (memory of how to do something, such as how to ride a bike) that is distinct from declarative memory (memory of informational content, such as text of a speech). When we connect movement with information, we activate both types of memory, and our recall is more accurate as a result. (p. 54)

Keeping this in mind, as you explore the materials in the Montessori 3–6 classroom, you'll want to note not only the types of learning activities that are available, but also how children's movement in the classroom and, more specifically, the opportunity to manipulate the materials on the shelves help to solidify their learning. "When we're engaged in physical activity . . . the visual system becomes more sensitive when we are actively exploring our environment. When our bodies are at rest—that is, sitting still in a chair—this heightened activity is dialed down" (Paul, 2021, p. 45). Movement and learning are inextricably linked.

Overview of the Practical Life area. One of the first areas of the Montessori classroom children are drawn to is Practical Life. Here children engage in activities that hold value to them because they reflect what they see an adult doing during day-to-day interactions at home and in their community (Gettman, 1987). From the moment we wake until the end of our day, we adults engage in endless tasks to maintain our lives. From the care of our physical selves to the maintenance of our homes, the social interactions we engage in within our community and workplace, to the food we prepare to sustain ourselves and our families, these are the activities that "sustain life, create culture, and build community" (Ramani, 2013, p. 49), and these are the essential elements of Practical Life in a Montessori classroom.

Curated materials in Practical Life allow children to scrub a table, slice an apple to either eat as a snack or serve to friends, button a jacket, polish a silver cup, sew a button, and care for classroom pets and plants. These exercises "give the child a sense of being and belonging, established through participation in daily life with us. Through Practical Life the child learns about his culture and all about what it is to be human" (Philipart, n.d.). These shelves hold trays containing bowls and tongs, spoons, eyedroppers, and small scoops to transfer dry or wet materials, such as beans or water. One tray may hold all the materials needed to wash a table or one's hands, including a child-sized apron, pitcher, bowl, sponge, soap, and small towel. Several small glass vases are available on a nearby shelf, along with a larger vase filled with beautiful flowers children can select from to create small table bouquets, adding to the beauty of their classroom. Other activities include wooden dressing frames (Table 4.1) that encourage children to practice fine motor skills using buttons, zippers, and snaps that will further their independence as they can ready themselves for the day without adult assistance.

STUDENT REFLECTION

Metal insets, sandpaper letters, practical life works, knobbed cylinders, wooden pencil holders, rolling rugs, loved having lessons, sometimes they'd be at circle time, how everything around me would fade away when I would concentrate, I would be in my own world, I could repeat something as many times as I wanted.

—Saasha, age 51, Montessori student 3 years

What exists on classrooms' shelves reflects children's lived experience within their culture, home, and community. What constitutes an artifact of culture depends on context: where we live, the language we speak, the clothes we wear, even down to the utensils used to feed oneself. In one classroom, a spoon or tongs will be used to transfer beans or seeds from one bowl to another, but in a different community context, chopsticks may be used to transfer items. Teachers take great care in curating materials, guided by Montessori's (1948) observation that when a child is self-sufficient, when he can tie his shoes or dress himself, he also reflects joy, a sense of achievement, and human dignity derived from a sense of independence.

Consider the many steps in table-scrubbing work, the purposeful movement and dexterity needed to complete the task:

- A child begins by putting on an apron and then lays out the table-scrubbing materials in a sequence they've observed in an earlier lesson with their teacher: the mat, a scrub brush, a small pitcher and bucket, a sponge, a bar of soap, and a hand towel.
- The child will take a pitcher to a nearby sink to fill with water, then pour the water into the bucket.
- Next, they'll dip the small brush into the water and then move the brush along a bar of soap. Before they have even scrubbed one corner of the table, they have spent several minutes coordinating these initial steps.
- They'll begin to scrub the table, noticing the suds they've created and the fresh scent of soap.
- The child will then wipe the soap from the table using the sponge. Their efforts are coordinated between wringing the sponge over the bucket and returning to wipe the table in an orderly manner. They take a moment to admire their work. But the activity is not yet complete.
- Now the child must empty the bucket into the sink, dry each material, place the hand towel in a wash basket, retrieve a fresh towel, and finally reorganize everything on the tray to ready it for the next person's use.

In this single exercise, there were many opportunities to build gross motor skills as the child carried the tray with all the table-washing materials and traveled from shelf to mat to sink and back again. They also used small motor skills as they poured water from the pitcher, held the scrub brush, and dried the table. Activities that include multiple steps and purposeful movements in time "lead to increased order, coordination, concentration, and independence—the foundations of learning for Montessori. As such, the exercises are considered indirect preparation for academics" (Conesa, 2023). So yes, children learn to scrub a table, but they are also reinforcing mindful habits that will positively influence later academic learning.

Uma Ramani (2013) reminds us of two important concepts from Montessori's writings. First, Montessori intentionally referred to the materials in Practical Life as exercises and not activities. The materials would remain merely activities if their sole purpose was to teach children how to pour, scoop, wash a table, and so on. Although children do learn these skills as they use the materials, it's the value of Practical Life exercises when they are implemented outside of the classroom that elevates their purpose:

> It is through practical life that individuals find their place in the human narrative. The activities of practical life give us orientation, identity, and a sense of belonging. They give purpose and context to our lives as individuals. Education that is a preparation for life is meaningless without the context of practical life. It is what connects and locks the different parts into a meaningful whole. (Ramani, 2013, p. 52)

Montessori valued Practical Life exercises when children freely practiced a new skill in the classroom and then extended their learning by later applying these same skills at home or in their community.

HOW THE 3-6 MONTESSORI CLASSROOM SUPPORTS COGNITIVE DEVELOPMENT

> Maria Montessori understood that in order for children to construct themselves cognitively, ethically, and socially, they needed prepared environments and certain essential keys, so they could explore, order, name, and classify their world. For children under the age of six, she gave keys to the world in the form of sensorial materials. These "materialized abstractions" for color, size, length, weight, pitch, temperature, and so on are the keys for the child's mind to begin to classify their immediate natural and built environments.
>
> —Leonard, 2018, p. 38

Overview of the Sensorial area. As you move into the Sensorial area of the classroom, you will again see organized shelves containing two- and three-dimensional shaped materials for children to manipulate at a table or on a floor mat: a pink tower, brown stairs, red rods, knobbed and knobless cylinders, color tablets, and geometric solids, among others (Table 4.2). Each material engages learning through use of the child's senses (see Table 4.3). Montessori designed many of the materials,

Table 4.2. Sample of Sensorial Materials

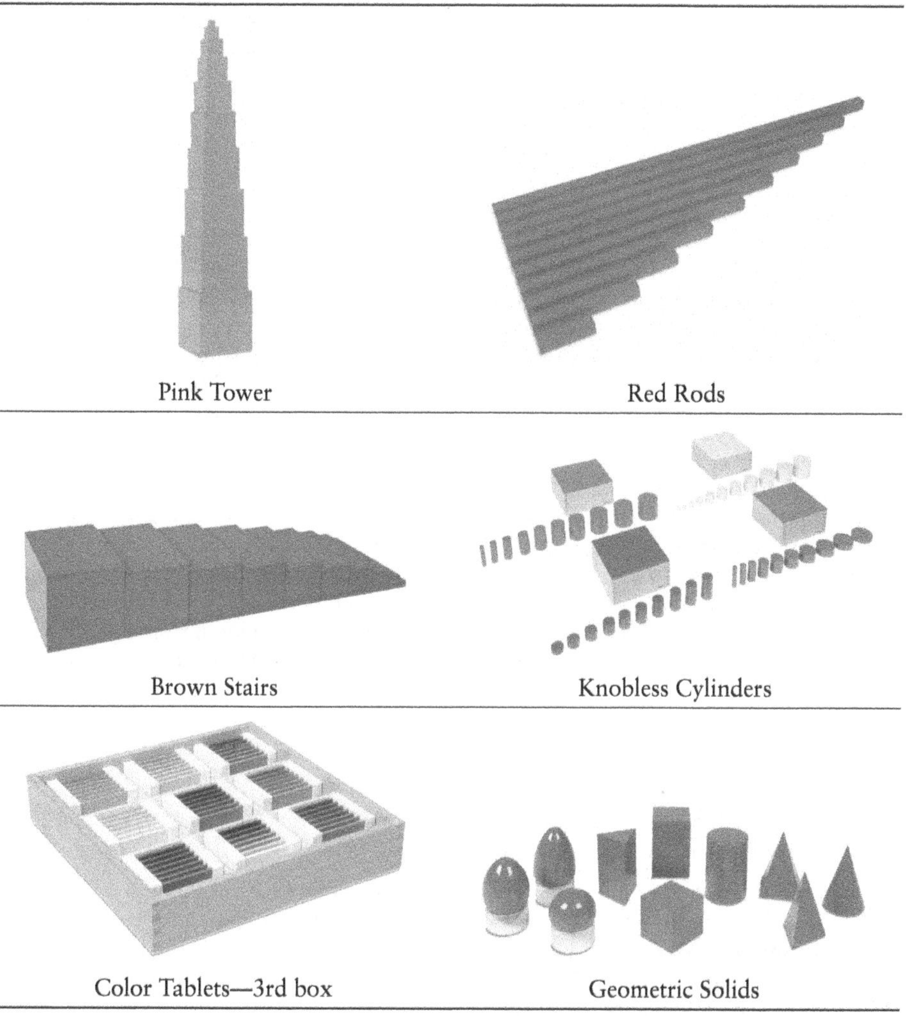

Pink Tower | Red Rods | Brown Stairs | Knobless Cylinders | Color Tablets—3rd box | Geometric Solids

informed by her predecessors, John Locke, Jean Itard, and Edouard Seguin, who shared a belief that knowledge comes through development of the senses.

Similar to the way children engaged with the Practical Life exercises described in the previous section, movement and activity are integral to the sensorial area of the classroom. Elizabeth Hainstock (1978/1986), in her book *The Essential Montessori*, describes children's engagement with Montessori materials and its influence on children's learning:

> Movement and activity are natural functions of childhood, and learning comes through them. Everything in the Montessori school environment is arranged to this

Table 4.3. Snapshot of Recent Montessori Research (from Brown et al., 2024, pp. 4–6)

Montessori: Evidence-Based Reading Curricula Brown et al., 2024	A study was conducted to determine if Montessori curricula met Arizona reading mandates. State ELA data demonstrated students enrolled in publicly funded Montessori schools scored significantly higher than their peers in non-Montessori classrooms with the greatest effects attributed to students enrolled in Montessori classrooms for 3 or more years.
The Long-Term Benefits of Montessori PreK for Latinx Children from Low-Income Families Ansari & Winsler, 2020	Study of over 5,000 Latinx children from low-income families who attended pre-K in Miami-Dade County compared 3rd-grade reading achievement for students who attended Montessori pre-K programs for one year to students who attended traditional pre-K programs. The Montessori group demonstrated better school readiness at the end of that one pre-K year and went on to score higher on measures of reading learning at third grade.
An Evaluation of Montessori Education in South Carolina's Public Schools Culclasure et al., 2018	The study analyzed public Montessori programs in South Carolina from 2011 to 2016. When compared to non-Montessori public school students, public Montessori students were more likely to have met or exceeded the state standards. Children from low-income backgrounds enrolled in public Montessori schools outperformed their peers in reading and improved more than demographically similar non-Montessori students.
Students of Color and Public Montessori Schools: A Review of the Literature Debs & Brown, 2017	Summarizes research on academic achievement for students of color in Montessori. The vast majority of studies reviewed found positive outcomes in reading for these students.
Academic Achievement Outcomes: A Comparison of Montessori and Non-Montessori Public Elementary School Students Mallett & Schroeder, 2015	Montessori students' reading scores in grades 1 through 3 were not statistically different than those of their non-Montessori counterparts. However, in grades 4 and 5, the reading scores statistically favored Montessori students.
Standardized Test Proficiency in Public Montessori Schools Snyder et al., 2022	Aggregated test score data from 195 Montessori schools in 10 states were compared to scores from its surrounding district. Montessori students were more likely to be proficient on state reading tests, and opportunity gaps were significantly smaller in Montessori schools.

> end, with a wide assortment of materials and the freedom to move about. Activity becomes increasingly important to develop, and the young child needs many opportunities for observation, movement and exploration. It is movement that starts the intellectual working. Manipulative exercises involving the use of the hand and mind together make the child an active participant in his own learning process. (p. 64)

Learning is supported by movement, meaningful activities, and agency. Children sit at tables or work on floor mats by choice, not at prescribed times. There are a multitude of meaningful activities to interact with, rather than worksheets to complete. Children have agency to self-select activities that are of interest to them (Figure 4.2), rather than focused on a single topic dependent on a scripted curriculum.

Marlene Barron (1983) described the stages children passed through when using Sensorial materials. First, they enter the exploration level, characterized by open-ended examination and use of materials. "Children need to view, touch, carry, smell and taste materials" (p. 9), which is the very design of Montessori materials at this stage of development. They have concrete experiences of abstract concepts. Next, children enter the imitation stage as they are encouraged to replicate a lesson as it's presented by the teacher—or as Barron (1983) suggests, perhaps working with another student who has experience with this material. The third stage is the initiation level, where the goal is to support children's creative

Figure 4.2. A Four-Year-Old Using the Knobless Cylinders in an Exploratory Way

and logical use of the materials. Often identified as *variations* of a lesson, children develop new patterns using the same material. Or they will develop *extensions* of a lesson, organizing two unrelated materials to develop a new meaningful pattern. For example, when using the color tablets, the child might identify other items in the classroom that match in color (e.g., a red color tablet matches the red-colored pencils found near the Metal Insets). And finally, the child moves into the pattern completion level, demonstrated when they use memory skills to replicate a pattern they developed on a previous day, or when one child begins a pattern and another child completes it. Each of these stages is important to children internalizing sensorial concepts, moving them from concrete to more abstract thinking.

Description of materials in Sensorial area. The materials were designed to help children organize their impressions of the environment by refining their senses as they explore their world. As discussed previously, Dr. Montessori recognized that before the age of 6, children are able to almost effortlessly take in important information related to their culture, language, and community, referring to this stage of development as the "absorbent mind" (1967/1995, p. 26).

Lessons are initially modeled by the teacher using very little dialogue so the child can focus on each step of the activity: how the material is carefully removed from the shelf, the manner in which it is used so as to appreciate the objectives embedded within the material, and how to then return it to the shelf ready for the next child's use. The teacher's movements are precise, and her gestures highlight key points of interest related to the height, width, weight, color, or tone of that specific sensorial material. Paul (2021) describes the power of gesturing as a method to embody abstract ideas:

> Gestures don't merely echo or amplify spoken language; they carry out cognitive and communicative functions that language can't touch. Where language is discrete and linear—one word following another—gesture is impressionistic and holistic, conveying an immediate sense of how things look and feel and move. (p. 69)

As you watch a Montessori teacher offer a 3-year-old child a lesson with the Pink Tower, you'll observe how she moves slowly, placing each block on top of the next, as if to compare size, deliberately gesturing and modeling the steps of the activity.

Specific vocabulary related to concepts learned through the materials are then reviewed in subsequent lessons. For example, in later lessons with the Pink Tower, children will still construct a tower, but they will also learn the words *cube* and *tower*; and comparative language such as *large/larger/largest* and *small/smaller/smallest*. The teacher will explicitly compare through gesture the largest cube with the smallest cube by physically moving the cubes to reinforce these concepts.

> Research demonstrates that gesture can enhance our memory by reinforcing the spoken word with visual and motor cues. It can free up our mental resources by "offloading" information onto our hands. And it can help us understand and express abstract

> ideas—especially those, such as spatial or relational concepts, that are inadequately expressed by words alone (Paul, 2021, p. 70)

It's the interaction of the Sensorial materials, the gestures and actions depicting the use of the materials, as well as the specific words attributed to the lesson that all serve to promote children's development.

This is a sampling of Montessori Sensorial activities including the Knobless Cylinders and the Geometric Solids.

The Knobless Cylinders (Table 4.2) are a set of four wooden boxes, each containing 10 knobless cylinders that vary by some combination of height and diameter. The cylinders in Box 1 (red) decrease in diameter with the height remaining constant. The cylinders in Box 2 (yellow) decrease in both height and diameter. In Box 3 (green) the cylinders decrease in height while increasing in diameter. And the cylinders in Box 4 (blue) decrease in height, but the diameter remains constant.

Knobless Cylinders are designed to support children's visual acuity of dimension as they order the cylinders by height or diameter. When presenting the red Knobless Cylinders lesson, the teacher will carefully remove the box from the shelf, carry it to a nearby table, remove the lid and place it under the box. She will then remove each of the cylinders and randomly place them on the table and pause. Knowing this box focuses on changes in the diameter of each of the cylinders, the teacher will intentionally select the two extremes—noting the cylinder that is the thickest and the one that is the thinnest. She will then let the child know that she is going to place the cylinders in order saying, "I'm looking for the thickest cylinder" from the remaining cylinders as she places each in order on the table in front of the child.

Geometric Solids are a set of 10 three-dimensional objects that are smooth and painted blue (Table 4.2). They support children's visual discrimination of the geometric forms and in later lessons, the further development of their stereognostic sense that began with the mystery bag at the toddler level. An example of its use is when you put your hand in your backpack and, without looking in the bag, locate your car keys. The geometric shapes include a cube, sphere, cylinder, rectangular prism, square-based pyramid, triangular-based prism, ovoid, ellipsoid, triangular prism, and cone.

The first presentation is done with two children on a mat on the floor. The solids are carried to the mat in a basket. Sitting across from the children, the adult removes the first solid from the basket and looks it over, using gentle hands to explore it. An important part of this exploration is to consider how it moves (or not!) when pushed a little. The basket is then shared with one child, then the other, for them to explore forms they select, too. Then the solids are returned to the basket. That is enough for one day. On a following day, the solids are now classified after separating the sphere and the cube on separate sides of the mat. As you retrieve a geometric solid from the basket, ask the question, "Does this go better with the sphere or the cube?" Classify the remaining geometric solids in this way. On another day, lessons may include introducing the names of the solids and playing games to increase retention through repetition. Subsequent lessons

Figure 4.3. A Three-Year-Old in the Sensorial Area of the Classroom

include the introduction of two-dimensional bases to match with the geometric solids. Lessons can be made more challenging by asking children to either close their eyes or use a blindfold to retrieve a geometric solid from a drawstring bag, relying only on their tactile sense to identify the shape.

The sensorial materials help children to organize and categorize their understanding of the world. They also help to build precise and descriptive language skills and serve as introductions to math concepts (Figure 4.3).

HOW THE 3-6 MONTESSORI CLASSROOM SUPPORTS CHARACTER DEVELOPMENT—KINDNESS AND CURIOSITY

Kindness and curiosity are two character traits nurtured in the 3–6 classroom. Kindness, the actions or speech that are intended to help others (Duckworth, n.d.-c), is an explicit outcome of many Grace and Courtesy lessons that are part of Practical Life exercises discussed earlier in this chapter. Many Practical Life exercises can be found on a shelf, framed within a carefully organized tray containing all the materials required for a child to successfully apply their new skills (pouring, scooping, tying shoes, etc.). However, this is not true of Grace and Courtesy lessons that are instead embedded within the classroom experience:

> There is not a specific physical area in the environment dedicated to grace and courtesy: you won't find it on a shelf; grace and courtesy has no specific materials; it is not tied to any particular time of the day or to any particular season of the year, nor is it

> directed towards any particular age or type of child. Rather, grace and courtesy is present in every area of the environment. (Sackett, 2015, p. 115)

Lessons that support children's self-development include: (a) learning to wash one's hands and face, (b) brushing hair, (c) polishing shoes, (d) folding clothes, (e) learning when to say "please" and "thank you," (f) how to offer a chair to a classroom visitor, and (g) how to ask permission to join another student's work (Gettman, 1987, p. 42). It was Montessori's belief that learning these acts of grace and courtesy would create "a positive and harmonious human society, the intended birthright of every human being" (Sackett, 2015, p. 116).

As an example, a Grace and Courtesy lesson might be the guide modeling how to greet someone at the classroom door. This might happen when an observer comes to sit in.

> *Guide:* "Hello, welcome to our classroom. What can I do for you today?"
> *Observer:* "I'm here to observe your classroom this morning."
> *Guide:* "Yes, we've been expecting you. There's a chair ready for you beside the classroom library."
> *Observer:* "Thank you so much."

As children become more familiar with these interactions and more confident in their Practical Life skills, they may also offer a glass of water to the observer.

Grace and Courtesy exercises are about much more than the tasks themselves. Montessori anticipated that these lessons would serve as preparation for children to be engaged with others in their classroom, home, and community. After much practice, children will have rudimentary skills needed to begin their role as active global citizens. "Grace and courtesy provide the foundation for young human individuals to experience and practice the skills of living in a manner based upon respect, dignity, and grace" (Sackett, 2015, p. 116)—qualities that support kindness and character development.

The 3–6 classroom also promotes children's curiosity, their desire to know more (Duckworth, n.d.-d), through the Montessori cultural lessons, as an example. The Cultural materials are the true heart of the Montessori curriculum. Here, children explore geography, history, and physical science, raising their curiosity about all that the world offers.

> The new aspects of child behavior that came to light through Montessori's work clearly demonstrated for the first time that children have an inner need to learn to know themselves and their world: to develop their intelligence and other mental functions through purposeful activity, to develop control of their movements through the use of their bodies in specific structured situations, to organize the contexts of their experience according to the order they encounter in the world, and, finally, through acquaintance with the property of things, to grow familiar with their environment and with their own capacities in order, eventually, to become independent. (Mario Montessori, 1976, p. 11)

Given the growing research demonstrating positive academic and non-academic outcomes of students enrolled in Montessori classrooms across diverse settings (Table 4.3), it's important to remember that Montessori's vision of education extended far beyond children's math and reading skills. Rather, her work remained deeply rooted in a pedagogy of peace, global understanding, and stewardship (Montessori, 1949/1964; Moretti, 2022) nurtured through the Montessori cultural materials. For instance, children explore a small globe they can hold in their hands. The continents on the first globe are made of sandpaper, while a later lesson introduces a globe with continents painted different colors so they can physically and visually experience the land formations and the oceans that surround them (Table 4.4). As Dr. Montessori shared, "we give the little child the orbis terrarum, the globe of earth made so that it can fit in his small hands. This is your home we tell him" (Leonard, 2015, p. 107). And so begins the exploration of their world—and their quest to find their place in it. Additional cultural

Table 4.4. Continent Study Progression (Adapted From Seldin & Raymond, 1981)

Montessori Material	Cultural Lesson
Globe 	• Sandpaper Globe • Painted Globe • Geographic location • "Here is where we live on this globe." • "And Isabella just started school with us. She and her family are from Columbia, South America, which is right here on the globe. They took a plane that took them all the way from South America to where we live." (Teacher traces path with finger.)
Continent Map 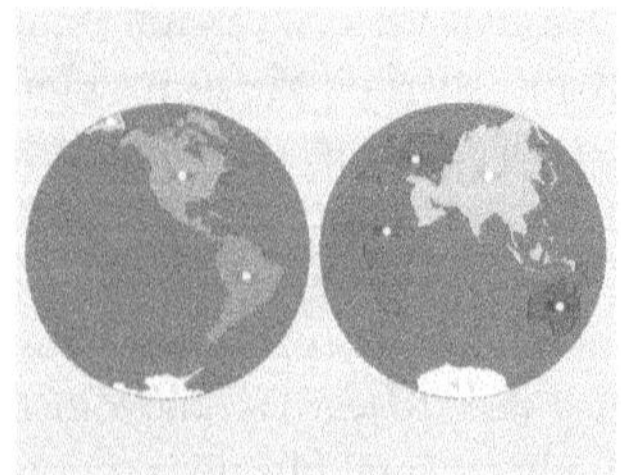	• Children learn names of each of the continents. • Learn where they are located on puzzle map. • Match puzzle piece (continent) and re-create on a control map (outline tracing of world puzzle map). • Extension: Children can re-create the continent puzzle by tracing each of the continents on the same color construction paper (red = Europe, green = Africa). Young children who are not yet adept at using scissors may punch-pin the shapes. Then the child re-creates the map on a large paper that has been previously painted to represent the ocean(s). Or they can create a continent booklet with a single page dedicated to each continent. • Children read/label each continent and corresponding ocean.

Montessori Material	Cultural Lesson
Europe Map 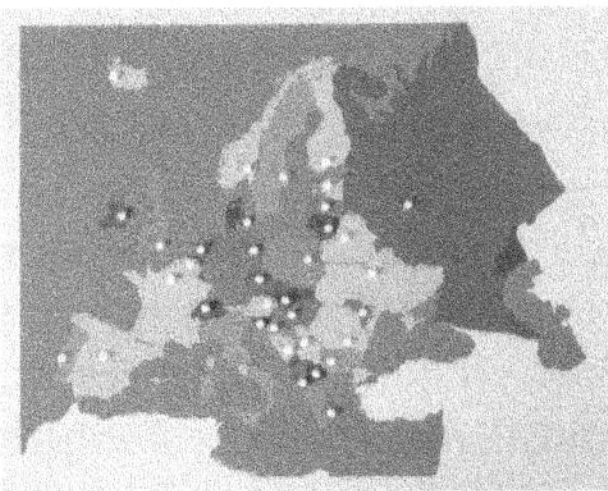 (there are individual maps for each continent—see suggested sequence below*)	Children are introduced to the • Continent of Europe and learn the countries that make up that continent (Ireland, Ukraine, Spain, Italy, Norway, Belarus, etc.) • Flags of each of the countries • Rivers, capitals, etc. • Languages that are spoken • Children may learn phrases from representative languages • Other cultural highlights: traditional clothing, traditional folk dance, food, homes, landmarks, plant life • Famous individuals: peacemakers, musicians, authors, artists, etc.
	• Famous artists and their paintings • 3-part cards of artist and their work • Famous musicians • Instruments and music specific to that region play during class time • Famous authors and their children's books • Add image of author to library with copies of their children's books shared during read-aloud. • Teachers create Continent Boxes that hold samples of materials representing countries (small dolls, postcards, pictures, souvenirs, etc.)

*Suggested order of map lessons: continent map, North America (you will present the continent where your school is located) and the map of the United States, South America, Europe, Africa, Asia, Oceania, and Antarctica.

materials, including lessons in geography, history, and life sciences. Geography is described in the next section.

Geography. Montessori classrooms have:

> retained geography as an essential discipline that is introduced in early childhood . . . [including] political, physical, economic, and cultural geographies . . . we find that children from a very young age are really interested in studying the map of their world and the people, landscapes, flags, animals, famous buildings, and so on from those far flung places. (Leonard, 2015, p. 102)

Tim Seldin and Donna Raymond (1981) in their book *Geography and History for the Young Child* present two objectives for offering geography lessons to 3-to-6-year-old children in Montessori classrooms: "to help her develop a clearer sense of spatial orientation through enriched and intensive interaction and experience . . . (and) to encourage her to become aware of and accept other cultures through related experiences in cultural studies" (p. 25). A Continent Study progression is outlined in Table 4.4. Adapted from Seldin and Raymond (1981), it offers an overview of the breadth and depth of learning in this area of the Montessori curriculum.

Puzzle Maps. After children are introduced to the world represented by its three-dimensional form using a handheld globe, the teacher will offer a lesson to bridge children's understanding of the globe and its two-dimensional representation using maps. They first learn the names of the continents, then the countries of North America. In the same manner, they learn the countries located on each continent. There's also a puzzle map that helps children to locate and name each of the states within the United States. Big work for a child who has not yet entered elementary school!

These lessons offer young children opportunities to build spatial awareness—where they are in relation to others throughout the world—while simultaneously building cultural awareness as we examine the homes, food, celebrations, family structures, and lived experiences of children around the world. In Montessori classrooms, children are offered the big picture followed by the details of a topic. Rather than beginning with the child's local neighborhood or town, geography lessons in a Montessori classroom follow the sequence of "earth, continents, countries, America, state, city, neighborhood" (Seldin & Raymond, 1981, p. 28). These lessons spark children's curiosity to learn more about their world, which will later become foundational work in the elementary classroom.

If we wish to build children's curiosity, we must be cautious to not narrow our focus in education. Like Montessori, we must offer them the world in its entirety. Not just "subjects and curricula useful for jobs and careers in a growth-oriented economy . . . [Rather] we must continue to teach connection and connectedness between peoples, humans and nature, our past and our future" (Orr, 2018, p. 48). This is our greatest role as educators, to prepare our children "to become 'radical professionals,' people of irrepressible courage, creativity, joy, and humility dedicated to the causes of life, justice, truth, decency, and democracy" (Orr, 2018, p. 49).

THE ROLE OF THE ADULT IN THE 3–6 CLASSROOM

The role of the adult in a 3–6 classroom is informed by standards set by several organizations that align to Montessori's vision. Highlights of recommendations from the Association Montessori Internationale (AMI, n.d.-c) require educators to meet the developmental needs of children in 3–6 classrooms by offering activities that support their independence, that allow for open-ended exploration, and that also lead to the refinement of children's movement, language, and intellect. The adult's role is to guide children to take a positive, pro-social role in the world.

And the American Montessori Society's School Accreditation Standards (2023) similarly require early childhood educators to facilitate a curriculum that integrates "the core areas of Practical Life, Sensorial, Math, and Language, as well as the Cultural Subjects. [Requiring] the learning environment [be] student-centered and self-directed" (AMS Standard 3.3.2, p. 3).

These Montessori specific requirements mirror professional standards and competencies outlined by the National Association for the Education of Young Children (2020), requiring educators in conventional classrooms to:

- be knowledgeable of children's development and learning and . . . able to apply this knowledge to their teaching.
- develop partnerships with families valuing their diverse needs.
- formally observe children's interactions in the classroom. These observations serve as assessments of children's learning and development, informing their readiness for particular lessons with Montessori materials and activities.
- be knowledgeable and able to integrate academic content into the early childhood curriculum. They organize and revise their curriculum and instruction in response to their ongoing observations of children's interests.

Student Reflection

I have to say the most memorable aspect of my Montessori classroom has always been the teachers. They all made a lasting impact on me, whether it was their positive approach to teaching or the experiences they gave me.

—Courtney, age 46, Montessori student for 7 years

Montessori educators are the crux of what occurs in the classroom. "It's the role of the adult in a Montessori classroom to support natural development, so it's our adult responsibility to learn as much as we can about how the children develop, so that we can recognize and remove obstacles to that development" (Huneke-Stone, 2015, p. 85). Montessori educators are continuously balancing what should be included on a classroom shelf, as well as what must be removed. When a material is no longer of interest to the children, if it has missing pieces, or if the activity has not been carefully thought through in advance of its use in the classroom, then the educator must make conscious edits to their classroom.

As Huneke-Stone (2015) pointed out, Montessori believed that educators must "encourage children to eagerly and respectfully explore and examine the world they live in [and] we need to create the psychological climate that encourages exploration" (p. 9). Similar to indicators found in the Classroom Assessment Scoring System (Teachstone, 2023), adults support a positive classroom climate when they are aware of the individual needs of children, display warmth and respect, nurture positive relationships through calm interactions, and explicitly model how to properly use materials.

Educators recognize the importance of these early years and the special aptitudes available to young learners. The study of child development offers educators a template to prioritize the design of relevant activities. In practice, each child's individual needs are considered so that educators can better navigate the trajectory between where students are now and design a path to what comes next. The three-period lesson is an instructional strategy Montessori educators use to individualize lesson presentations. Each period, or stage of instruction, allows children to demonstrate their understanding of the lesson. During the first period, for example, the teacher introduces the lesson, modeling the material using only the language needed to convey the concept of the activity. The second period is an opportunity for the child to practice the activity with support from the teacher, serving as a formative assessment of the child's learning thus far in the lesson. The third period of the lesson asks the child to conduct the lesson without support and serves as a summative assessment of their learning (Zoll, Ansari et al., 2023; Zoll, Feinberg et al., 2023).

The three-period lesson mirrors facets of the I Do-We Do-You Do model of instruction (Archer & Hughes, 2011) frequently used in contemporary classrooms, but there are differences that may significantly influence children's learning. For example, in a conventional classroom the I Do-We Do-You Do instructional approach is usually delivered and assessed during whole-class instruction. A specific lesson on vocabulary or a math strategy is introduced by the teacher (I do), practiced by the students with support from the teacher (we do), and then students re-articulate key learning objectives of the activity (you do).

By comparison, the Montessori three-period lesson begins as an invitation to an individual student or a small group of 2–3 children. The first period of the Montessori lesson and the I Do portion of the conventional lesson share a similar instructional approach as the teacher models the introductory lesson for the student. It should be noted that Montessori educators place a greater emphasis on modeling the introductory lesson versus narrating through the content. The second and third periods of the lesson allow the Montessori educator the opportunity to hear each individual student's response to assess learning, which is not always possible when a lesson is delivered to the entire class. When a student demonstrates that they have not yet mastered the lesson objective, a teacher in conventional education will provide "immediate corrective feedback" (Archer & Hughes, 2011), while a Montessori educator will simply thank the child for working through the lesson, noting to revisit the lesson again the following day. These follow-up opportunities reinforce concepts not yet understood by the child, allow time for additional practice, or perhaps take a step back to a previous lesson to reinforce foundational concepts. This is the We-Do portion of the lesson, where the child practices new concepts with the support of the adult. The You-Do portion of a Montessori lesson demonstrates a gradual release to the student moving from You-Do with support of the adult, as needed. Then this is followed by

You-Do independently, as the child demonstrates readiness to use the material on their own, working toward mastery (Fisher & Frey, 2021).

Rather than the curriculum leading children through daily and weekly instructional schedules, in a Montessori classroom it is the child and their response to the activity that informs the teacher's instructional dosage: how often a lesson is revisited and practiced, and when they are ready to move forward to the next learning challenge. From the moment a teacher introduces a new lesson, they have made many instructional decisions based on observations of their students' progress during the 2-to-3-hour morning work cycle. Children have uninterrupted time, agency to direct their learning, and ample opportunity to engage with materials to practice new skills as they work towards mastery. This model of individualized instruction requires that teachers balance their instruction to

> constantly guard against over-teaching or over-correcting—correcting a child who is unaware that he has made an error and intervening to show a child how to improve a skill he has barely learned. Respecting at all times the child's right to help himself and to solicit help only when he feels it is needed. (Rambusch, 1962/2012, p. 76)

When educators adjust their instruction, make decisions to present the lesson again the next day or perhaps revisit a foundational lesson to reinforce key concepts from a previous lesson, teaching shifts to not only ensuring student learning, but to also preserving students' right to dignity in learning.

CHAPTER 5

The Montessori 6–12 Classrooms

> Education between the ages of six to twelve is not a direct continuation of that which has gone before, though it is built upon that basis. Psychologically there is a decided change in personality, and we recognize that nature has made this a period for the acquisition of culture, just as the former was for the absorption of the environment.
>
> —Maria Montessori, 1948/1955, p. 3

> The sphere of cosmic education is complex as it considers each aspect of a person in relation to every other living form on the planet; it includes the history of the world, of the cosmos, and of our role in it. By extension, it includes the history of civilizations and cultures, elaborating a holistic vision of phenomena. The goal of this philosophical framework is the activation of an education tending towards universal cooperation, the affirmation of democracy, of peace, and the construction of a new world.
>
> —Montessori, 1949 as cited in Raimondo, 2023, p. 29

TWO 6–12 CLASSROOM VIGNETTES

Montessori classrooms for 6–12-year-olds are usually referred to as Lower and Upper Elementary classrooms. The Lower Elementary consists of those students who are 6- to 9-year-olds and Upper Elementary serves 9–12-year-olds.

> The wisdom of the 3-year cycle, that opportunity to move from first-year newbie to second-year experienced to third-year mentor in all areas—social, emotional, academic—while building on previous experiences, applying previous knowledge, and seamlessly moving into new levels, is one of the most effective and successful elements of a Montessori program. This is especially true for children in their tween years, since few children develop at the same rate in both social and academic realms (Breiman & Coe, 2016, p. 48)

The children of both classrooms display the same priorities and characteristics as explained later in this chapter, but those in the first group are just learning to navigate their newfound social community and intellectual work while the older students are now more comfortable being a part of a group and are easily engaged in their personal intellectual growth.

Lower Elementary (6-9-year-olds)

It was 10:10 in the morning. There were two adults and 24 students in the space. One small group was working outside—I could see them through the wall of windows—and I was told that others were in "Garden to Table," the program for students that has them working in the garden and the kitchen, making today's lunch for the class.

The room felt homey—lived-in, busy, creative, and resource-rich. The students were together but doing things in groups of two, mostly. There were lots of math materials out, including the checkerboard and large bead frame, fractions, and racks and tubes. In the middle of the room were two very long timelines—one was the timeline of human beings and the second, which was not yet labeled, seemed like it was on its way to being something important, too. Students were drawing on it. There were also a few piles of what seemed to be cardboard building projects. No one was working on them while I was there, but they had their own space and were definitely student-made.

There were smiles and laughter coming from one small group, but all students in the classroom appeared to be productive in their respective work. The adults could be heard, but the tone of their voices was collaborative and curious. No single voice could be heard above others.

The guide gave an introduction lesson on the checkerboard (a tool for long multiplication—see Table 5.1) to two boys on the big rug in the middle of the room—among 15 other children all doing their own thing on floor mats and chowkis (floor tables). The Assistant supported a child using the large bead frame (like an abacus) also for long multiplication.

Another member of the faculty appeared at the door. He was greeted with a hug from one of the children, said a few words to the Assistant, and then some children got up and left the room with him. They were going off to the garden for some ecology work. A short time later, a reading specialist poked their head in and recognized that the child he needed to work with (the one working on the multiplication problem with the assistant) was already engaged in work. The adult left so as not to interrupt the child.

Another child was being read a message on the board by an older child:

Write three ideas you remember about the timeline of human beings.

The young child was unable to start. The older child tried many ways to scaffold the younger one's thinking. The guide was aware and acknowledged the effort of the older child. No words were needed, just a nod of the head let them know they were seen.

After a few minutes, though, the young child appeared to be getting a little emotional. The guide noticed and sat down beside her.

"Can I help get you started here?" The child nodded and listened as the guide spoke in a calm and caring voice.

"Let's go look. What do you see? This timeline doesn't have a visible title, but if it did, it would be the timeline of human beings—of people. Tell me something you see."

"This man is eating meat with his hands. They are going to get dirty," the child replied.

The guide continued, "Interesting, we don't really do that do we? What do we use?"

After the child responded, the teacher continued, "What else do you see?"

The child responded, "He has hardly any clothes"

"Oh, that's true!"

"And there is ice here—so isn't he cold?"

The teacher smiled and nodded.

To conclude the discussion, the teacher remarks, "Wow, that is a lot of stuff you found. Are you at a place where you could write something down?"

The child nods—and heads off with a look of determination on her face. I overhear the child talking aloud. She states her points as she writes them, searches and recalls vocabulary that was discussed, and sounds out parts of words as she writes. There is even some self-promotion. "That's right," the child whispers to herself.

The phone rings. A child answers it.

"Hello, LE2 here."

"Yes, one moment please."

The child walks over to the Assistant.

"Alma—it's for you!" And then walks away with purpose.

Next is an excerpt from an Upper Elementary class—4th, 5th and 6th grade. The increased maturity is apparent in their communication and the topics for discussion are appropriately also more advanced.

UPPER ELEMENTARY (9-12-YEAR-OLDS)

There are beautiful original paintings on the big walls with high ceilings. The room felt efficient and productive. There was an "Algebraic Equations" lesson near a whiteboard with nine students participating. The lesson was nearly over. All students were engaged. Two of the nine were sitting on the floor with a floor table but listening and speaking too.

The guide checks in with each child in a natural manner, making sure they each understand the content. The guide reminds them to show their work with the practice questions.

One child says—"I figured out I could do it this way." The guide responds—"Well, you got to the same answer, so that's totally fine."

Another child says—"I totally get it! The hard part is showing your work!" The guide agrees with a nod.

As the lesson concludes, the guide asks one who is packing up their things—"What will you do next?"

There are other spaces in this upper elementary classroom of 9-, 10-, and 11-year-olds. In the center, in addition to many plants, there is a long bench seat by a window and a few tables where students are working alongside a support aid who is keeping them on track to finish their individual work choices. The bench holds four others eating snacks and drinking out of water bottles. The talk is about science projects and soccer.

In a third space, a guide explains a chart to the children and on the whiteboard behind them are the words **Infiltration and Fusion Migration,** written in cursive. The chart displays what looks like billiard balls in different arrangements. There are six students sitting at the table with the guide. The instruction feels more like a conversation. Questions are asked and explanations are offered by all. The discussion starts abstract and becomes personal.

"My grandmother came from Argentina, and this was what happened to her."

"That's right, it just might be. She brings her traditions to you and your whole family, and then you bring some of those traditions to us at school. Just as in fusion migration, the culture comes with you and everyone benefits. Like the holiday we celebrated yesterday!"

The kids shout, "St Patrick's Day?"

"Right, that is the day the Irish people celebrate coming to the U.S. It is very popular, and many people wear green and eat Irish food on that day . . . as well as on other days of the year."

"Let's make a definition!" The guide begins to talk while writing on the board.

"Infiltration and Fusion Migration is when a group of people visit a new area, and they see the success of the people living there. Some of the visitors may move on, but others stay."

The guide stops to say, "Feel free to paraphrase or put this in your own words. That is good note-taking practice."

Then the guide continues, "Those that stay, settle in a friendly way, that's not to say there is no conflict, they maintain some aspects of their identity and take on some traits of the new culture and vice versa."

She gives other examples of this migration—the Hmong people in Minnesota and the first Hmong U.S. Olympian Gymnast. Then the guide shifts the discussion to be led by the students.

"So what might be some benefits of this kind of migration?"
The students continue,
"There's less violence?"
"More celebrations?"
"Added culture!"
They get it.

THE ELEMENTARY STUDENT IN THE 6-12 CLASSROOM

Over the first six years of life the child has self-constructed their "innate potential for characteristically human functions: biped locomotion, the use of the hands, language, a reasoning mind, the capacity to choose" (Ramani, 2023, p. 136). They have benefitted from extended periods of concentration with freely selected materials worthy of their attention. They have explored endless examples of beauty found in their environment, and through their senses have learned to organize an ever-growing registry of information.

Now, between the ages of 6 to 12, the child enters the second plane of development. There is a marked transition from concrete to abstract thinking. Students demonstrate a deeper intellectual ability and are able to reason through more complex problems. There is a shift in social priorities as they seek to find their place among peers. These social tendencies help them to understand their role and responsibility as a member of a classroom community. Instruction, in response to this social tendency, includes lessons delivered through intentional interactions with other students so together they may reach their full potential. Stories, elaborate narratives with grand gestures and exciting people, are a vehicle for learning. Lessons emphasize the contributions of individuals and groups of people to help students envision themselves making a difference in the world.

In conventional elementary classrooms, instruction is routinely standards-based though there's abundant evidence of effective teaching that instills "deep, authentic, and accelerated learning starts with students . . . [focusing] on topics relevant to their lives . . . guid[ing] students toward new and deeper knowledge and more sophisticated skills" (Pianta in Blumenthal & Pianta, 2024, p. 5). Pianta highlights studies of student motivation measured in conventional classrooms that "shows them starting to disengage around 4th grade, a decline that shows up even earlier and more seriously for students from historically marginalized backgrounds or who have struggled to learn basic skills in prior years" (2024, p. 5).

For students to be highly motivated and engaged at this stage of development requires relevant learning opportunities with challenging content they can deeply explore. "They like group work, organizing and negotiating with each other. Children deliberate over right and wrong, good and bad. They have boundless curiosity about origins of things and connections among things. They feel kinship and empathy for all living things" (Maier, 2023, p. 153). Topics around emotional experiences are essential. "Feelings of real affection, of caring for other living beings, emotions of tenderness, gratitude and wonder . . . [as well as] encounters via the intellectual disciplines, through biology, biogeochemistry, taxonomy" (Leonard & Allen, 2021, p. 86) are found throughout the elementary curriculum. Students aim big, working towards answering the perpetual question on their mind, "Why?"

The elementary child flourishes within a prepared environment that offers opportunities for independence, such as the simple act of their answering the phone in the Lower Elementary Vignette. Just as there are notable shifts in children's development, the learning environment now extends beyond the classroom as students' learning expands into the local community.

Physically, children are more capable than they were in early childhood, demonstrating increased fine motor skill. These refined skills will now have practical application in the classroom. At this age, children do not benefit from prolonged periods of confinement sitting at a desk, so physical movement must be an integral part of learning. Cognitively, the elementary student is primed to exercise their greater intellectual capacity. They continue to have interest in the correct words for new concepts and seek to know the reason for things. To strengthen the heart, will, and mind at this stage, the environment must have at its core, through all of its systems and resources, a goal of process versus product, internal versus external motivation, and collaboration versus competition. The child who has entered the second plane of development will absorb these values through the social space of the classroom and learn lessons of independence, interaction, and interdependence within it.

Student Reflection

I remember doing science experiments like food decay, composting, and using a microscope. I remember the racks and tubes, doing book reports and doing a survey on everyone's favorite color for the entire school. I remember putting on plays, having potlucks for the school community, and digging holes at recess.

—*Cecilia, age 36, Montessori student for 7 years*

ENVIRONMENTAL RESPONSE TO DEVELOPMENTAL NEEDS (6-12)

It's important to note that the mixed age groups found in Montessori classrooms offer many benefits for children. For example, the youngest students moving up from the Children's House observe the many activities used by their older classmates. Students will of course have the support of the Montessori educator in the elementary classroom, but with diverse age groups situated in one classroom, there's also opportunity to access the knowledge of peers to support student learning. Sometimes an older peer can explain a new concept in a way that's heard more clearly by someone in the same social grouping. It's apparent how multi-age classrooms can benefit younger students, but mentor peers also benefit in this leadership role. First, though they may have already "mastered" content, explaining concepts or offering lessons can reinforce and sometime unlock new perspectives on learning that may in turn influence future learning. In addition to supporting cognitive growth, these mentoring experiences support the mentor-student's social-emotional or character development, reinforcing kindness and authentic purpose (Duckworth) by making a meaningful contribution in the classroom

The classroom space will be busy, and it will not be quiet, especially at the lower elementary level. The observer will note the many different activities and lessons happening simultaneously in the classroom. Though there may be some time given to whole group discussion, most classroom time is devoted to small group learning. To the untrained eye, the guide will appear to be "spinning plates" as they simultaneously support many students in their learning across multiple subjects all at once.

The classroom, as mentioned previously, is specially prepared by the adults for this age group in response to who they are developmentally. A broad curriculum meant to support intellectual skill development is implemented, while also offering students a big picture of the world, inspiring wonder and awe. Through imaginative images and provocative stories, seeds are planted, and a plethora of background information is offered throughout these 6 years.

To help the reader visualize the complexity of the Montessori elementary curriculum, we share the Hexavium chart (Figure 5.1, use the QR code to access PDF of image) developed by Terry Millie, a Montessori educator and teacher trainer from Canada. Using blue triangles from the geometry materials, he was inspired to design this image at the conclusion of his elementary training in Bergamo, Italy. The image depicts the depth and interconnectedness of the elementary curriculum. At the center of the hexagon is the individual child with six learning paths to explore during their six years in the elementary classroom. Each path begins with an inspiring Great Story that illuminates subject areas and reveals topics for further exploration and knowledge. Subject areas move beyond math and language to include geography, history, and biology. Art, Music, and Physical Education, as well as a second language acquisition, are also complimentary parts of the program, though they are not included in this chart. As stated in the previous chapter, conventional classrooms rely on separate published curricula to cover content across all learning domains at each grade level. In a Montessori classroom, an integrated spiral curriculum is used, meaning there is an interrelatedness to what is being learned, and any topic can be explored at different depths depending on the developmental needs, interests, and individual strengths of the students. The complexity of the Montessori curriculum provides opportunity to revisit topics from different perspectives and across multiple years to further allow students to master content.

Figure 5.1. Hexavium: A Visual Representation of the Montessori 6-12 Curriculum Developed by Terry Millie

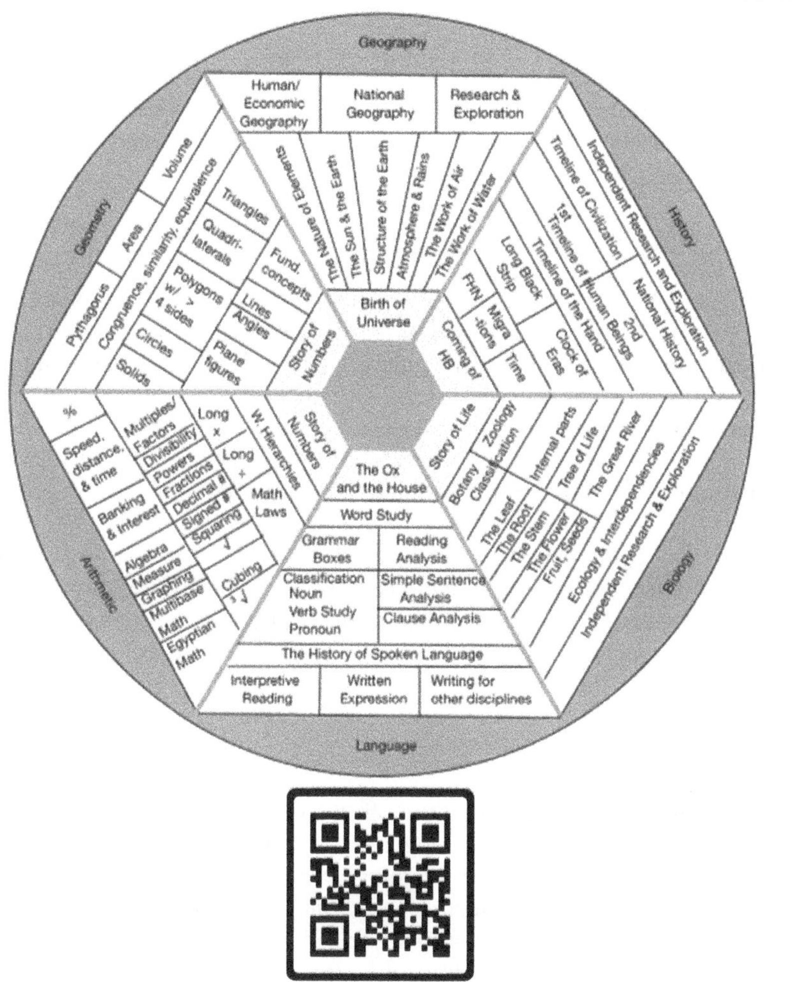

In addition to providing an organized visual of the elementary curriculum, the Hexavium offers a template for planning lessons. It can be used by the educator to ensure that there's variance and balance in the curriculum that's delivered. The template can also serve as a self-assessment tool for students to monitor their own learning by asking themselves: Where have I explored, where have I not explored, and what else can I learn? These acts of self-reflection, metacognition of what they have accomplished, and freedom to choose where to move next in their learning build children's sense of agency, while also enhancing decision-making, planning skills, and self-confidence. These are mighty learnings that will exponentially influence future experiences.

Student Reflection

I recall an emphasis on developing independence in this period. Much of the work and extracurricular activity was geared at students operating on their own as much as possible.

—Dan, age 26, Montessori student for 11 years

Cosmic Education. At the core of Montessori's cosmic education is an understanding that what unites us is foundational to a world where we coexist in peace. Developmentally, these new social beings are particularly attuned to contemplate such a big idea. Their social development begins with an appreciation of others using materials and activities, stories, timelines, and charts that create a sense of wonder in all that is available in the world as they are introduced to the values and contributions of civilizations and individuals throughout time on our planet.

> The sphere of cosmic education is complex as it considers each aspect of a person in relation to every other living form on the planet; it includes the history of the world, of the cosmos, and of our role in it. By extension, it includes the history of civilizations and cultures, elaborating a holistic vision of phenomena. The goal of this philosophical framework is the activation of an education tending toward universal cooperation, the affirmation of democracy, of peace, and the construction of a new world, (Montessori 1949 in Raimondo, 2023)

The elementary Montessori curriculum offers the whole of the universe to inspire children and create a sense of belonging to the world, saying, "we shall walk together on this path of life, for all things are a part of the universe, and are connected with each other to form one whole unity. This idea helps the mind of the child to become fixed, to stop wandering in an aimless quest for knowledge. He is satisfied, having found the universal centre of himself with all things" (Montessori, 1948/1955, p. 6).

There are five Great Stories, each designed to help students understand the organizing principles of the universe. Each one serves as the introduction to a field of study. The first story, The Birth of the Universe, gives students an introduction to how the universe was organized and is the beginning of Geography and Earth Science studies. The Coming of Life story introduces interdependencies between nonliving environments and all living entities and starts students thinking about Biology. Through the story of the Coming of Human Beings story, students learn that humans have been present for only a brief but meaningful period of history, relative to the rest of the universe. The Story of Communication in Signs (sometimes told through the story "The Ox and the House"), introduces students to the history of written language, an invention connecting us to the thoughts, ideas, and experiences of others, and serves as a path to further explore Language work. Finally, the Story of Numbers highlights the varied approaches to number systems humans artificially constructed to represent elements of daily life, and this begins work in Mathematics and Geometry. These stories are appealing to the students because they begin to explain the reasons behind the work they will engage in each day. They offer children an overview of the traditional subject areas from a humanistic viewpoint as a way to orient themselves in their daily work. The elementary students begin to understand their world, learning that humans are just a single aspect of what makes the universe and that we all have a significant role in its ongoing existence. As children are introduced to these concepts, they unconsciously sense that the purpose of their work is twofold: to learn about the universe and contribute to it based on their interests, their growing sense of self and responsibility, and the inherent need for global stewardship.

The environment must include the necessary materials needed to perform a task. Classrooms must include the equipment and consumables necessary to successfully follow the demonstrations and experiments that follow imaginative stories in the Geography and Biology areas. Having everything that is needed is very important for building children's independence. Preparing the environment for the work that will be done is, initially, the adult's job. But as the children mature into the Upper Elementary class, they realize they can take on the responsibility of preparing the environment, too.

There are natural elements in the physical space of the classroom. A variety of plants and animals offer authentic opportunities to practice kindness through care. Students learn to observe and note when plants need tending or when the fish need to be fed. With the responsibility of caring for other living species, children grow an appreciation for the symbiotic relationships established through these cohabitations of species in the classroom.

STUDENT REFLECTION

I remember the grammar boxes in elementary school. This helped me understand grammar on an elemental level. I remember my first introduction to grammar with the demonstration of the black noun pyramid, a concrete thing, and the red verb sphere, symbolizing action.

I remember every material turning abstract or somewhat conceptual topics into tangible, engaging ways to learn. For example, in elementary the pin maps allow students to actively learn geography in a way that is memorable. The floor letters (idk what they're called) show Children's House students that letters are quite literally the building blocks of words, and they have the power to put these together.

—Sarah, age 20, Montessori student for 12 years

As in the Children's House classroom, the Montessori materials stand out for their exactness, their beauty, their brilliance in design, and their self-correcting ability to support student learning. Many of the elementary materials extend concepts learned in the Children's House classroom through new applications that deepen knowledge of content (Figure 5.2). For example, the bead chains as described in the Children's House vignette offered practice in linear counting in the 3–6 class but are now used to understand squaring and cubing of numbers in the elementary classroom. Some materials use shape and size to express relationships among them. For example, the Geometric Hierarchy of Number materials (Figure 5.3) illustrate the categories of numbers from units to millions. The unit is a tiny cube. The 10 is a bar of tiny cubes. The hundred is a square of 10 bars, and the thousand is a cube made of 10 squares. The colors are consistent. Green is unit, blue is 10s, red is 100s. This goes for the units of the thousand family, 10 thousand and 100 thousand. Note the giant green cube. That is the unit of the million family. These materials are mathematically exact, and one million of the unit cubes make the million cube.

Large colorful charts accompany many lessons to engage students through their imaginations in the great intellectual work they will do. Connections between lessons and classroom materials are essential at the elementary stage because they support student motivation prompting discovery and reason that will fuel future deep learning investigations. These charts are readily accessible to the students in the classroom—if not on display to support a recent lesson, in a box—organized by topic for students to pull out and refer to in their follow-up work. Some of the timelines have a complementary blank timeline and separate pieces of drawings and words that can be put together like a puzzle. These are aids for understanding and memorization.

Figure 5.2. Student Working With the Iron Material to Explore Congruency, Similarity, and Equivalence

Figure 5.3. The Geometric Hierarchy of Number

Student Reflection

I vividly remember the Great Lessons and stories. I imagined the giant dragonfly on the Timeline of Life as being as big as a car and was disappointed as an adult to learn that the giant dragonflies of the Carboniferous Era were only as big as seagulls! My friend and I drew a life-sized Triceratops (or maybe to scale?) and it took forever to color it in! I loved imagining the Ice Ages and seeing them represented on the timeline . . .

—*Annie, age 46, Montessori student for 10 years*

Curricular Areas. The elementary Montessori curriculum offers a variety of lessons across all domains, with a focus on connectedness among living things. Gratitude for the contributions of people and civilizations all over the world is emphasized. Though there may be some variation in teacher training, there is consistency in the breadth of content available to students in the 6 years of the elementary program. And the elementary guide will augment the curriculum to complement the interests of the children, as well as to meet local standards and educational requirements.

As outlined in Millie's Hexavium, there are six subjects in the curriculum: geography, language, history, biology, geometry, and mathematics. Each subject is seeping with interesting facts and rich vocabulary and is introduced through a big-picture vision that is then explored at greater depth through detailed analysis. As a spiral curriculum, many topics are introduced in the early years, then built on through the years that follow, so that subjects are revisited and children's understanding is deepened. Children easily become interested in the topics when they know a little about them already.

HOW THE 6–12 MONTESSORI CLASSROOM SUPPORTS PHYSICAL DEVELOPMENT

From this age until they reach puberty, the rate of physical development begins to decelerate, and students grow approximately 2 inches annually (Gallahue et al., 2012). The Montessori classroom during these years continues to focus on physical skills with more specialized movements and adequate time to master these skills—notable because sports and games become an essential element to the social life of elementary children. To meet these needs for movement, the Montessori elementary environment now expands beyond the physical classroom. Students gain experience by going out on planned trips in their community. Learning now occurs in two settings, in the prepared environment of the Montessori classroom as well as the world beyond the school. Learning is place-based as students explore nature and community settings. These diverse settings serve as a "universal syllabus" informing both teaching and learning (Leonard, 2015, p. 98).

In the classroom, there is freedom of movement within the learning cycle, with multiple options for seating. Children may be on a big rug on the floor or in a rocker by the books. There are tables to conduct group work and single spaces to accommodate individual preferences. A comfortable child is more able to concentrate on the work in front of them. Students explore beyond the classroom; they're able to experience the physical difference of learning spaces throughout the school. They may go outside to play a drum, work on a picnic table, or walk to the art space to grab some paints (Figure 5.4). Movement may include a visit to a local zoo to observe giraffes through the "going out" program of the classroom. Of

Figure 5.4. Elementary Students Drumming Outside

course, with these freedoms of movement, systems are in place for accountability and communication.

The lessons themselves involve movement. Students are responsible for gathering all the necessary materials needed for lessons and follow-up work. You'll note small groups of students participating in the work of the lesson, from initiating the lesson to its completion as all materials are returned to their rightful place on the shelf. Lessons also involve materials that require manipulation to illustrate new concepts. Students will physically slide two isosceles triangles together to form a rectangle or manipulate four congruent right-angled triangles to make a square. Additional materials from the geometry curriculum are discussed in the next section.

The Geometry Curriculum is a great example of how movement is integrated into learning in Montessori elementary classrooms. By having materials to explore and test, a child learns by doing. There is no need for fidget toys when fidgeting with materials is purposeful and brings conceptual meaning for the child. As an example, manipulatives used in a lesson on angles begin with a group of 4–6 students in a Lower Elementary class. They've previously been introduced to their study of polygons and have an understanding of lines and angles and the corresponding language. Notice in the following dialogue, the increased complexity of this elementary lesson, the built-in language, participation, practice, choice, and formative assessment.

- The guide begins on a corkboard using two sticks attached at one end. One is fixed with a tack holding it stable, and the other (on top) can move in a circle.
  "This is an angle," she says as she moves the stick.
  "This is an angle." She moves the stick again, a little further around.
  "What is this?" she asks as she looks at the students expectantly.
  "An angle," students say in unison.
  "Right—you've got that.
- "Okay, but let's get more specific." The guide moves the top stick to 90 degrees of the bottom stick and pulls out a "measuring angle." (This is a laminated 90-degree triangle with the right angle marked in red.) She carefully places it in the space between the sticks and looks at how it fits.
  "This is a right angle. It fits perfectly! We call this a right angle." She writes the words *right angle* on a label facing students so they can see it.
- Then, she moves the stick to make the angle larger and asks the students, "Is this a right angle?" She puts the measuring angle in and waits for an answer.
  "No," the children respond.
- The stick is moved again to put a more significant space between them. The measuring angle is put in.
  "Is this a right angle?"
  "No."
  "Why not?"
  "It is bigger!"

"Exactly! When an angle is larger than a right angle—as shown with the measuring angle—it is called an obtuse angle!" She writes the word *obtuse* on a label and shows it to them.

- "Okay, but what about this?" She moves the stick to make an angle smaller than 90 degrees. She picks up the measuring angle and asks:

  "Is this a right angle?"

  "No."

  "Is it an obtuse angle? Is it larger than a right angle?"

  "No. It is smaller."

  "Exactly! This is an acute angle."

  She writes *acute* on a label as she says, "When an angle is smaller than a right angle, it is called an acute angle. This is an acute angle!"

- "Okay—everyone tell me what kind of angle I make. It might be a . . . right angle, or it might be an obtuse angle, or it might be an . . . acute angle." (This is the formative assessment phase of the lesson.)

  The guide has them all call out as she makes one angle in front of them with the sticks and uses the measuring angle for support.

- Then everyone is handed a measuring angle and two sticks and they try themselves. They can even make their own labels to use.
- Afterward, for application of concept, the group walks around the room and searches out examples of all three angles. These can be found at doors and picture frames, table legs, etc.
- Follow-up exercises on another day may include a child repeating this lesson on their own or presenting the same lesson to another child who has not yet received the lesson on the three types of angles. One student may make a visual chart of the angles with labels, and another may search for materials in the outdoor environment using the measuring angle or try to explain the different kinds of angles in words—to reinforce their new knowledge.

HOW THE 6–12 MONTESSORI CLASSROOM SUPPORTS COGNITIVE DEVELOPMENT

Individualized Learning. Because Montessori education is considered a spiral curriculum, skills are revisited and developed across age spans, making it possible for students of any skill level to successfully take part in Montessori elementary classrooms. Unlike students in conventional education programs, Montessori students do not collectively complete the same grade-level lesson during a particular time block within the classroom schedule. Lessons in a Montessori classroom are individualized. This means that students progress at their own pace, selecting materials that are of interest to them, with support offered as needed. If a child entering a Lower Elementary classroom is not yet reading with fluency, they can still participate in grammar exercises by partnering with a child who is able to read.

Parallel to this work, the child would also continue build reading skills. In between group lessons with their guide, students will select activities they would like to work at each day based on previous lessons they've received. This creates more opportunity to reinforce learning by revisiting materials while working with friends at the same time. The educator's role is to determine where the child is in their learning and to meet the student where they are by offering lessons each day that advance learning in manageable increments. Extra support is available throughout the work period by the assistant, the guide, and peers.

STUDENT REFLECTION

I often think of the ways we learned math with the materials because I feel like those methods have always stuck with me. It trained my brain to think a certain way from the very beginning, and I attribute that to how successful I was able to be throughout the rest of my educational journey.

—Megan, age 24, Montessori student for 7 years

Mathematics. The elementary Montessori math curriculum supports cognitive development in three ways. It uses materials to explain concepts, offers various materials for repetition of needed skills, and covers a broad array of topics (see Table 5.1), offering endless paths of study for each child.

The math materials are brilliantly designed, and using them brings a deep understanding of numbers and quantities. The materials help students visualize numbers, quantities, and equations. Students can see why their answer is correct and the steps that were needed to arrive at the conclusion they chose to solve. Using the materials first, without writing everything down, isolates the concept for better focus and understanding. As they work through the numerous exercises within the lessons, the concrete materials in time shift into written steps. Over time, students move toward abstraction, and are able to complete difficult math concepts without the need for materials. Multiplication facts are committed to memory through different materials such as the large bead frame, the checkerboard, the bank game, and the flat bead frame (Table 5.1), which extend students' practice of multiplication facts in long multiplication. By having many paths to the acquisition of these facts, the work remains interesting and repetition is natural.

Table 5.1. Various Materials Used for Learning Multiplication in the Elementary Classroom

Large Bead Frame	Checkerboard	Bank Game	Flat Bead Frame
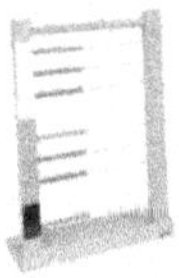			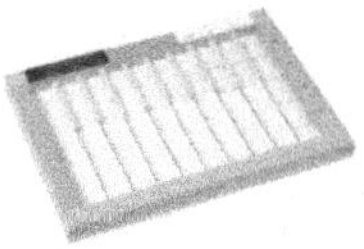

The exercises in the elementary math area are broad and cover topics that are beyond the scope and sequence of conventional schooling at this level (Table 5.2). Some examples are the introduction to algebra, numbers with different bases, and cubing a trinomial. The students coming from the Children's House have already been introduced to base 10 categories—unit, tens, hundreds, and thousands; counting; and have a strong impression and basic understanding of the four operations (addition, multiplication, subtraction, and division.) Now it is time to expand on this foundation by increasing the scope of numbers and turning early impressions into a deep understanding of mathematical concepts. The areas of math study and the individual topics are listed in Table 5.2. The reader will note that though a single topic is listed, there may be numerous exercises within it to support students' deepening conceptual understanding within that topic.

As you can see, there are endless possibilities of lessons on an immense number of math topics to foster students' cognitive development, at a pace that meets individual students' learning needs.

STUDENT REFLECTION

I remember the rooms being very calm. I also remember learning long division when I was in 2nd grade in a way that just made sense. Relearning it later on in public school around 5th grade was so confusing by comparison. I remember feeling engaged in what I was doing because I was able to be self-directed and explore my interests.

—Hannah, age 33, Montessori student for 7 years

Table 5.2. Elementary Math Topics

Area of Study	Topics Covered
Introduction to Mathematics	Why humans need numbers
	Categories and number families
	Measurement
	Word problems
Long Multiplication	Multiplier, multiplicand, and product
	Category multiplication
	Cross multiplication
	Word problems
Commutative and Distributive Properties	The commutative property—order of digits doesn't matter in a multiplication or addition problem.
	The distributive property is the idea that when you multiply two numbers by two numbers, you must make four calculations and then add them up.

Area of Study	Topics Covered
Multiples and Factors	Multiples Lowest common multiples Factors
Long Division	Distributive division Group division Divisibility of numbers to find patterns Word problems
Squaring and Cubing I	Prerequisites to squaring Notation of squares Notations of cubes Games for squaring and cubing The decanomial square The paper decanomial Exercises for squares and cubes Word problems
Fractions	Fractions as equal parts of a whole or a unit Introduction to the notation of fractions Equivalence of fractions Simple operations with fractions Addition and subtraction with different denominators Exercises leading to abstraction (+,–) Multiplying by a fraction Division by a fraction Word problems with fractions
Decimal Fractions	Quantity Symbols linked to quantity Formation and reading of quantities Operations with decimal fractions Conversion of common denominator to decimal Multiplying or dividing numbers by the powers of 10 Multiplying a decimal fraction by a decimal fraction Relative size of terms in a multiplication problem Relative size of numbers when dividing Division of a decimal by a decimal Steps to abstraction on paper Word problems

(*continued*)

Table 5.2. (*continued*)

Area of Study	Topics Covered
Squaring and Cubing 2	Transforming a square Passing from one square to another Squaring a sum Squaring with hierarchical value Cubing a binomial Cubing a trinomial Cubing a quadrinomial Cubing with numerical value The Story of Three Kings Cubing a number with decimal value Word problems
Square Roots and Cube Roots	Square roots Notation of square roots Cube roots Notation of cube roots Word problems
Other Topics	Powers of two Powers of three Powers of 10 Distance, velocity, and time Principal interest, rate, and time Introduction to algebra Operations using exponential notation
	Expanded power notation Operations with exponential notation Negative numbers Non-decimal bases Conversion from one base to another Ratio and proportion Word problems

For those students who have not yet secured some of the foundational math concepts discussed in the previous chapter, there are opportunities to ensure that students secure this content so they may begin math work in the elementary classroom. Additional support may be needed in numbers and notations, categories of numbers, introduction to the four operations, and math facts. These topics were offered in the 3–6 class, but in a different way that was developmentally appropriate for that age.

HOW THE 6-12 MONTESSORI CLASSROOM SUPPORTS CHARACTER DEVELOPMENT—GRIT AND GRATITUDE

Montessori education, at its core, recognizes young people as already viable members of society. Through progressive opportunities to develop independence offered in Montessori classrooms, students have an established identity beyond their family unit. They are able to develop and express their own personal thoughts, beliefs, style, and characteristics, which further influences their growth as a whole person. Expectations for how students and educators will interact with each other are established early in the school year. Community meetings are also held weekly to air issues, discuss solutions, and show gratitude for others. In these spaces, all voices are heard, and challenges are resolved with the support of others.

Put simply, the elementary classroom builds students' character development through its classroom culture, systems, and expectations that allow each child to flourish and realize their full potential. Every child has agency in this individualized approach to learning and development—but they also have responsibility and accountability to complete their work. Grit (Duckworth, n.d.-e) is a natural component of meeting individual goals. The elementary classroom also nurtures another human characteristic, the development of gratitude. The curriculum emphasizes the contributions of individuals and diverse civilizations across time. Through a broad array of human studies, charting how each fulfills their human needs, students grow an understanding and appreciation for all of humanity.

Grit is a passion and persistence for long-term goals (Duckworth, n.d.-e). Long-term goals, though, are relative to age. For an adult, a long-term goal may be buying a house in 10 years. For an elementary student, revisiting a project multiple days to completion, looking through an array of resources to research a topic, or working through many arrangements to prepare for a going-out trip can all serve as authentic opportunities to develop grit in the classroom. Daily, students learn to persevere in a 3-hour morning work period. With larger projects, students may need to revisit goals and readjust timelines over the course of weeks or months until their project is complete. To meet long-term goals, students will demonstrate grit when things don't work out as they imagined in their choices, collaborations, and in completing follow-up (practice) work after lessons. These executive function skills are nurtured when students have opportunities to make their own choices and have responsibilities where they are always engaged (and sometimes fail) within the classroom environment. They build resilience. In the 6 years of the elementary program, students practice and make progress toward skills needed to be productive and happy learners. This process happens one child and one goal at a time.

A work journal can help students develop grit, as they learn to record and self-monitor their work in the classroom. Journaling provides insight into their productivity, helping students notice when revisions in time management might be necessary. As described previously, the Hexavium, a visual representation of the subject areas and topics presented in the elementary classroom, can also be used by students as a self-assessment tool, helping them see where they spend their time and where more focus may be needed in their studies. As students grow and learn, the weekly meetings become times when failures are discussed, adaptations are arranged, and new goals are set to offer alternate opportunities for success by the child. These meetings are more collaborative between guide and student at the Lower Elementary level and become student-led in Upper Elementary.

"Going outs," the student-planned opportunities to further engage their studies outside the Montessori classroom setting, are another example of classroom protocols that support students' executive function skills. Destinations for these trips out of the classroom come directly from the students' interests, and they are responsible for making the arrangements using a framework provided by the adult. The trips are for intellectual or practical reasons and require students to fill out planning forms, make phone calls to secure a chaperone, or gather details about the destination that might be necessary to successfully plan for the excursion. "Going outs" offer a very real and relevant way for children to safely fail. If all of the parts are not in place, a trip will not happen. That is the logical consequence. This opportunity for real-life consequence allows for some disappointment but also for there to be growth in resilience and perseverance to ensure that future requirements are met.

Gratitude, or appreciating what you have been given (Duckworth, n.d.-f), is a very important element in cosmic education (described earlier in this chapter). As already mentioned, students have a platform to share gratitude during community meetings each week. Offering this line of thinking into the group brings more and more appreciation for the little things that we experience.

Gratitude is a core value throughout the Great Lessons and other areas of the curriculum. The elementary history curriculum is an obvious way to highlight the development of gratitude in elementary students. Table 5.3, an annotated outline of core lessons, demonstrates the humanitarian focus of these history lessons.

Beginning at first grade, students grow their understanding of other people that serves as a foundation for further studies. Though not as common in conventional schools, global knowledge grows through the 6 years in these classrooms as stories are expanded and rich details are explored. The depth and breadth of the curriculum require that educators begin early with engaging narratives about our history and then revisit frequently throughout students' academic careers. In the Montessori 6–12 classroom, children learn about their world through discipline-based activities in geography, history, biology, and the arts. These cultural lessons "induct students into disciplinary thinking . . . [to interact with] this body of tested knowledge and skills that has been strategically built up over time by scientists and artists . . . [so as] to induct children into thinking about the world from the perspective of a geographer, chemist, or musician" (Hutchinson, 2013, p. 194). The objective is to prepare students to interact confidently in the world and to serve as stewards of the planet. Some may think it is too soon to share such weighty concepts with elementary students because the task of countering

Table 5.3. History Lessons and Inherent Messages

Lesson	Learnings
The Story of Life / The Coming of Life	This story expresses the wonders of the cell and how it carries life in many forms. As almost a parallel story to human history, it describes how cells used to perform all tasks themselves but later developed into groups of cells doing different jobs and working together to accomplish more significant tasks: the essence of cooperation.
The Black Strip	The primary purpose of presenting the story while slowly unrolling a very long piece of black fabric is to give the impression of the immensity of time that the Earth has been revolving around the Sun. At the end of the strip, which is revealed at the end of the story, is a tiny line of red ribbon symbolizing the relatively very short duration humans have been part of this timeline. It is a message in humility.
The Coming of Human Beings	This story reflects what had to happen for humans to survive on Earth and how they evolved over time.
The Hand Chart	The message of this story is that humans figured things out for themselves using observation and exploration.
The Clock of Eras	This presents a more detailed look at the relative time of the earth's existence and human life, and a review of the lessons above.
Fundamental Needs of Human Beings	This is a framework for the different aspects of human needs (nourishment, clothing, art, housing, etc.) with examples of how those needs could be met. All studies of people in the classroom use this framework as a start during the 6 elementary years.
Migration Charts	As humans began to move around on the earth, this shows how they organized themselves.
The History Question Charts	For deep dives into civilizations, these charts offer guiding questions under the topics of the nature of the country, practical activities of their citizens, and the intellectual and spiritual aspects of the culture and relations within various groups.
The Three Phases in History	These stories express history's Nomadic, Agricultural, and Urban phases.
The First Timeline of Human Beings	This timeline tells the story of humans before written language. It is sparse and focuses on the different peoples and how each group met its fundamental human needs. From here, students make shorter timelines about one need, like food, to demonstrate how that need was fulfilled.

(*continued*)

Table 5.3. *(continued)*

Lesson	Learnings
The Second Timeline of Human Beings	This timeline overlaps with the first but is dense with additional content and developments. These stories of progress evoke gratitude in the children for all the work that was done before them, that have informed what we appreciate and use in present history.
Four River Civilizations	These stories explore the people and the maps of Mesopotamia, Egypt, Indus Valley, and China.
New World Civilizations	The historic tales of the Aztecs, the Olmecs, the Mayans, and the Incas are introduced.
American History Timeline	These stories begin with offering a big-picture view of American history and later highlight the progression of civilization over time. This timeline serves as the basis for many stories about our history.

"ignorance, fanaticism, gullibility, fear, misogyny, racism, and violence" (Orr, 2018, p. 48) should be left to adults to manage. Rather, we must actually begin with foundational skills "early on in classrooms where the young learn the basic rules of democracy: critical thinking, honesty, fairness, empathy, nonviolence, and citizenship" (Orr, 2018, p. 48), skills that are the very essence of the Montessori pedagogy.

THE ROLE OF THE ADULT IN THE 6–12 CLASSROOM

The Association Montessori Internationale (AMI) requires that educators working with students from 6 to 12 years of age be responsive to students' curious minds, their ability to abstract and imagine, their moral and social orientation, and their energy for research and exploration. Elementary educators also

> build knowledge through an in-depth study of the world and how it works. Studies are integrated across disciplines that include geography, biology, history, language, mathematics, science, music, and other forms of artistic expression. Exploration of each area is augmented by the children, who organise visits beyond the confines of the classroom to gain real-life knowledge from community resources, such as the library, planetarium, botanical garden, science centre, factory, hospital, etc. This approach fosters a feeling of connectedness to humanity and encourages children's natural desire to make a contribution to the world. (AMI, n.d.-d)

Similarly, the American Montessori Society's School Accreditation Standards (2023) require elementary educators to facilitate a curriculum that integrates the core areas. Individually paced academic progress allows students to explore their interests and acquire the mastery of basic skills and knowledge.

> The learning environment is student-centered and designed to promote the development of organizational and time management skills, healthy identity development, conflict resolution, social justice, and anti-bias skills, concentration, independence, cooperation, and collaboration. Indicators of successful implementation include teacher guidance, assessment in planning in concert with student planning, monitoring, and assessing their own work, and demonstrating responsibility for their own learning and actions. (AMS Standard 3.3.3, pp. 3–4)

To meet these objectives, Montessori elementary educators are able to apply what they know about the developmental needs of their students across all domains. They model curiosity and enthusiasm for learning, see the good in every child, and approach each day as an opportunity for their students to begin anew. Lessons are well planned but flexible, so they are responsive to students' interests. Educators continuously observe and monitor learning and support their students to reflect on and self-assess their own work.

STUDENT REFLECTION

I remember my teacher Wendy really making the difference. She really encouraged us and taught us how to love school work. I remember friends asking why I still tried in school since there were no grades. That's what Montessori and Wendy gave to me, a passion for my work.

—Nick, age 22, Montessori student for 9 years

Educators also self-monitor to ensure that students remain at the center of their work in the elementary classroom. As in all Montessori classrooms, the adult understands the students' characteristics and support their growth through lessons and interactions, systems, and oversight, and by curating an environment consistent with the academic, social, emotional, and physical needs of these students.

> Good teachers understand what students everywhere can confirm: teaching is not just talking, and learning is not just listening. Effective teachers are able to figure out not only what they want to teach, but also how to do so in a way that students can understand and use the new information and skills. Furthermore, they know what students are ready for and need to learn, so they choose tasks that are productive, and they organize these tasks in a way that builds understanding. Finally, they monitor students' growth and progress so they can address specific needs and keep students engaged in school, learning productively, and growing as cooperative

> and thoughtful citizens who will be able to participate in society. (Horowitz et al., 2005, p. 88)

The elementary guide is interested in everything and conversational about many topics. When needed, they are ready to learn alongside their students. They are storytellers, dramatic and funny, calm but assertive. They are fair and consistent—and this consistency helps the students to understand established boundaries so they can learn freely within those lines.

The educator in the elementary classroom has a different task than those at other levels. This teacher must, with the help of the materials, ignite children's imaginations, support their need to work in groups, and inspire them to make the most of this significant time of intellectual growth. The guide continues to model orderliness during their instruction, but they balance the need for students to learn content versus neatness while they are deep in their work. The priority at this stage of development is not for students to be orderly as they work though new concepts, but for them to access all the tools they need to complete their task. Elementary students do not naturally repeat tasks as their younger selves once did. The guide needs to encourage them to practice skills through the scope of the curriculum, social interactions with peers, and novelty. The lessons aim to inspire through stories and big imaginative ideas. Games and drama also motivate students to repeat and replicate work to learn necessary concepts and skills.

Montessori recognized that children who had learned in 3–6 Montessori classrooms held an advantage as they entered the elementary classroom compared to their 6-year-old peers who did not have previous Montessori experience—and these differences would influence the educator. As Montessori points out in her book *To Educate the Human Potential* (1948/1955), students who were previously enrolled in the Children's House before entering the elementary classroom knew "how to read and write, [they had] an interest in Mathematics, Science, Geography, and History, so that it is easy to introduce [them] to any amount of further knowledge" (p. 7). Dr. Montessori continues to highlight what this means for the teacher, how much more prepared they must be for students who do not yet have this foundational knowledge

> The teacher's task is no small or easy one! [They] have to prepare a huge amount of knowledge to satisfy the child's mental hunger, and . . . is not, like the ordinary teacher, limited by a syllabus, prescribing just so much of every subject to be imparted within a set time, and on no account to be exceeded. (p. 7)

Dr. Montessori then offers reassurance, explaining that her scientifically based curriculum would build on what students already knew by providing them with a vision of the universe through her cosmic curriculum.

Montessori educators are grounded in the belief that learning is accomplished by the learner:

> The most significant research finding is deceptively simple: Learning is done *by the learner*. That is, as teachers we tend to think that our students learn on account of what we do. But that is a mistake: Our students don't learn because of what *we* do; they learn because of what *they* do. Our challenge, then, is to design learning experiences for students that are interesting and that yield the learning we desire. (Danielson, 2009, p. 36, emphasis original to quote)

STUDENT REFLECTION

I remember getting a lot of say in the projects I was working on. I could choose the topic of my persuasive essay or the time period I did my history project on. I remember garden-to-table lunch and being taught how to cook with what we were growing. I remember my teachers encouraging my love of reading. I thoroughly enjoyed the opportunity to be involved with MMUN [a Montessori-based United Nations project] and learned so much during those conferences. I also have fond memories of the field trips we took as a class. I remember hating my typing classes but being so thankful I did that when I transitioned to high school.

—Isabel, age 23, Montessori student for 11 years

Much learning and changing happen during the 6 elementary years. The adult's role is not solely to teach but to also support students in acquiring knowledge while trusting individual development and respecting all students as capable human beings. Individualized instruction is dependent on the educator's observations and connections to each student. Teaching and learning are holistic, not rigid. Mutual trust is established. The adult trusts the good intentions of children and recognizes their natural tendencies to be social at this age (Figure 5.5).

The guide curates the classroom environment differently in the elementary grades than they would during the first plane of development. They offer a greater variety of lessons and instructional approaches: an introductory lesson to the whole group, intentionally revisiting content through discussions, facilitating small-group lessons. There is an emphasis on proper language in all lessons, expanding background knowledge and vocabulary related to specimens and scientific elements, as examples. Everything in the environment holds learning value, and time, as always, is of the essence.

An elementary guide facilitates learning by connecting children to materials, supporting them in finding resources, and keeping the positive, individualized learning culture alive. An elementary guide tells stories, demonstrates materials, and models kindness, curiosity, and productivity. They model for children that mistakes are opportunities to learn. They cultivate a classroom culture by setting expectations for how the classroom functions, putting systems in place to guide the actions of both the students and educators.

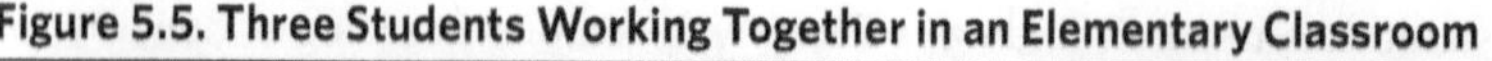

Figure 5.5. Three Students Working Together in an Elementary Classroom

Student Reflection

One of the most important parts of my Montessori education was learning to treat others with kindness and respect. The golden rule "Treat others the way you would like to be treated" is something that will always stick with me. Learning with physical objects as opposed to typical education was very helpful for me. For example, learning math with beads, geography with physical maps, etc. I credit my geography skills to this day with hours spent working with the maps. I remember my teachers being very caring and instilling important traits. I remember when we had to roll up mats they needed to be done very carefully and this contributed to my attention to detail.

—Tyler, age 27, Montessori student for 8 years

Elementary guides create a sense of belonging as they welcome students into the classroom each morning, perhaps shaking hands or engaging in a moment of connection and conversation. When children need a little direction, the guide might offer some suggestions. For children who have plans for themselves, the guide can show interest and offer support. For a child who is not yet able to settle into the day, the teacher is there to listen and offer direction to ensure their success.

Individual student-guide meetings are formal ways of monitoring growth and guiding future learning. Together, the teacher and the student meet with the student leading the discussion and review of work completed in previous weeks. This collaborative review brings awareness to both parties about areas of learning that might require additional practice, or it lets the educator know that the student is ready for next steps. The task of the Montessori elementary guide is to plant seeds of knowledge and ignite their students' interest in learning. The objective is not to achieve a perfect score on a test. Rather, practice makes progress. The educator's objective is to establish in their students a lifelong interest in learning and the resilience to move their knowledge and development forward. This will provide a foundation for the more complicated developmental phase that is to follow: adolescence.

CHAPTER 6

Montessori 12–18 Classrooms (Middle and High School)

> The adolescent must never be treated as a child, for that is a stage of life that he has surpassed. It is better to treat an adolescent as if he had greater value than he actually shows than as if he had less and let him feel that his merits and self-respect are disregarded.
>
> —Maria Montessori, 1948/2007, p. 72

What I love about Montessori

by Nieve B., *Mountaintop Montessori School, middle school student*

A world separate
From the average day
Filled with boxwoods and laughter
Young faces and new faces
Little people and tall people
Every color equal in a place of learning

I walk in
Greeted by people
Who want
To be there
A campus
Designed for the students
The teachers
I walk into classes that
Are
Different for each person
No matter the ability
Each met with
Classes that they can succeed
In
There is work
But I'm not

Drowning
I'm comfortable
yet
Challenged
I wish
This place could always be
My school
As it has been for the last 8 years
An intellectual
Refuge for me
And so
Many others

TWO ADOLESCENT CLASSROOM VIGNETTES: MIDDLE SCHOOL AND SECONDARY

Observations at the Adolescent and Secondary levels are difficult to capture with the same detail as observations recorded with younger students. Since adolescents have mastered learning using many of the Montessori materials, these observations now focus on the application of knowledge. The first observation takes place in a middle school classroom of 12–15-year-old students highlighting interactions and classroom systems that invite dialogue and create community to meet the developmental needs of these students.

Middle School

It was a Tuesday at 1:10 p.m., and a bright and beautiful room provided chairs with arm tables that held adolescents. They were seated loosely by gender, at their own choice, near and facing the front of the room; no books or computers were visible. They listened intently to an adult woman talking about biotech. She worked for a local company and explained that her background was in biology, and she currently works alongside a hundred others who find solutions to issues in the biotech field. She discussed practical problems that are solved through careful analysis, creativity, and science. Her work advanced military projects, as well as everyday life issues. She shared a technology that overcomes the middle ear's natural ability to provide equilibrium. With this technology, they can train fighter pilots to overcome the body's natural response, to better handle loss of orientation while flying. She delves into the details of other projects and then asks if there are any questions.

"Could this technology be used in the opposite way, to trigger the body to respond to a simulated misorientation on the ground as a training method?" Another arm goes up, another doozy.

"Good question," she says and then proceeds to answer it in a somewhat technical way.

At the end of the session, the speaker is thanked, and the students are informed about what will happen next and which educator they'll be working with for the afternoon. Half of the students are going to Permaculture work with Griffin, while others are beginning their study of ecosystems with Britt. They get up to stretch their legs and prepare themselves. This is a break for the students, but instead of giggling with each other, 11 students walk to the front to ask the guest speaker some additional questions that are relevant and demonstrate their engagement in the topic. After, they return to their seats and chat while they wait to hear from Britt. Once getting her bearings, Britt addresses them.

"We are moving on—that was a nice conclusion to our last topic of study, wasn't it? I noticed you were all very attentive, and I also heard many great questions."

"Today's plan is for Permaculture Group A to meet Griffin in the garden." (She refers to the written schedule on the SMART Board visible to the group.)

"This practical, hands-on work has great value in learning, and, as we heard from our guest speaker, can have significant value beyond your schooling in everyday life, so take advantage of this opportunity!" She smiles, and this prompts movement from group A—the others stay where they are.

The ecosystem group is half of the class, a mix of 7th- and 8th-graders. She points back at the agenda to outline the plan for the science group.

"Today we are going to do sitspots, an activity for the start of our Ecosystems study.

"So, who knows what *sitspots* are?" A hand goes up.

"Marilyn?"

"When you sit and observe around you."

"That's right—but there are a few ways to do this. One way is to simply be, which is beneficial for mindfulness and finding your zen. However, for scientific purposes, we approach it at a deeper level. When we do a sitspot for science, we have a few things in place before we go, and what we do while observing or after also comes into play.

"So, what do you think we do while we are observing for science?"

"Make a drawing or diagram?"

"Write words down describing?"

"Put labels on the diagram."

"Okay, but what do we use to capture those things?" Britt asks and the students add points.

"Your environment?"

"Your senses?"

"Paper and pencil?"

"Exactly!"

It all comes together.

"You should sit in your spot silently—"

"Right, silent how?" Britt questions. Students pipe up.

"In your body."

"With your voice."

"And mind."

Britt adds, "Yes, so your senses can notice things. Today's sitspot will be for 10 minutes. It might be helpful to look within 6–8 feet around you . . . However, I won't limit you, so if you must, feel free to look further. So during a sitspot, you write down or draw during that time, focusing your thoughts on the space and nature within it.

"We also want to think of things through a scientific lens, and our language will help us do that, so before we go, let's remember some terms that will be relevant in the follow-up activity. Who remembers what biotic factors are?"

Through discussion, the class defines this word as well as abiotic factors, consumer, producer, decomposers, omnivores, herbivores, and carnivores.

One student throws up a hand; Britt nods at them.

"Would it be possible for an adult human to live off only meat and water for a sustained amount of time?"

"Yes, for at least a few days. The length of time would depend on many factors, including your genetic composition. You will undoubtedly notice the difference in your body's performance." This generates lots of discussion.

Some children talk out, and others answer. When it becomes a little disruptive, Britt says, "Cecily, hold on, please." Her tone is matter-of-fact and not stern. Cecily stops talking over Ethan.

Some silly questions get asked; some serious ones, too. Britt answers as well as she can. Are we going out there for 10 minutes? Are we doing the diagram outside or inside? It all gets clarified.

When they go out to disperse, the ecosystem students take their tasks seriously and get started.

Up past the basketball courts and the chicken pen, there is a bench with the word *Kindness* written on it. Just behind the bench is a fenced garden where the Permaculture Group is actively engaged.

One girl is pulling weeds and preparing a tiny plot of soil along the edge of the garden. As she pulls, she tosses them into a wheelbarrow. A group of girls is heard chatting and giggling in the bunny house, and a group of boys returns from elsewhere with a tarp. The adult asks them to put it on the compost pile covered in cardboard. "Do you know why we do this?"

"To grow nutritious food?" someone responds. The adult explains that the tarp acts like a lid on a pot—it holds the warmth and energy in, allowing the work to be done more efficiently.

A girl comes forward with a pack of seeds. Another has moved on to get compost from an already tarped area with a shovel. She dumps the weeds under the cardboard. Together, the girls spread a light layer of compost and then sprinkle the seeds carefully around. Griffin (adult) comes by and engages the students about their work. "Looks great! Do you know what happens if they get planted too deep? They won't have the energy to grow. . . . So don't put too much compost on top."

"Okay," the girls say. They share the job, discussing the amount of compost they're using, then conclude they are done.

One boy approaches the guide. "I'm leaving at 3."

"Okay. We all are. That's in 5 minutes."

A group of boys who had managed the tarp now move on to watering in another corner with a hose. They get goofy, one sprays, one runs, and they laugh. They go back to the job.

The permaculture work is winding down. Some students who were caring for bunnies join the group. And the hose and wheelbarrow are returned to their respective spots for another day.

"Bye, Griffin!"

"Bye, guys! Thanks!"

As in the first and second plane, this third plane is a time of great change in development. You'll notice that the level of responsibility increases along with students' confidence, whereas the guide's support proportionally decreases while continuing to individualize based on the needs of each student.

Secondary School

It seemed to be a regular high school, until, as we meandered around the buildings under covered walkways, a chicken wandered through. There were actually many chickens, all going about their business. The guide, with expertise in Sustainable Agriculture, met us and offered a tour of the greenhouse. They described many projects under way and listed the animals cared for by the students; in addition to the chickens, there was a rooster, snake, dogs, goats, box turtle, and a beekeeping setup. The students had designed and implemented a hydroponic system for the plants that were grown in the greenhouse using tilapia to fertilize the plants and feed the fish. A watering arrangement was comprised of PVC tubing that ran the length of the building. There were experimental gardens, as well as space they used to grow collards for the community. The guide then led and welcomed us into the building and his classroom. It was a relaxing space with couches, warm lighting, and wooden shelves. The shelving created little nooks so that small groups could form but still be a part of a community-wide discussion. There was also what might have started as a little office off to the side, but upon peeking, it stored supplies and products in process for the students. There were bars of goat soap of different scents displayed on glass trays. There were also jars of honey, all produced on-site.

At one end of the classroom was a SMART Board and bulletin boards displaying practical charts like one that reserved a place for questions, who posed the question, and what was needed. The SMART Board displayed the day's agenda, announcements, and a clock. There was a *gardens* list that laid out steps of care: pick a garden, pull out old plants, put old plants in compost, add soil, add a square grid, and add plants.

The guide was working in a corner. Two students wandered in.

"What are you doing here already?" he smiles genuinely, and I sense a respect between the students and teacher.

"We don't know; we thought we could check on the animals," one said. She shrugs her shoulders.

"Okay, great! Can you also walk through the greenhouse and see how it all looks? We need to make sure the plants for the sale are all watered."

"Sure," one responded as they leave.

Over the next few minutes, singles and small groups come in, chatting pleasantly, finding their seats; one couple is holding hands. They take out their books and computers as they settle in; most share a greeting with the guide.

At 9:15 a.m., a tiny bell chirps from the SMART Board and Mr. Steven stands among the seated, not at the front, more like in the middle. He says hello to everyone and goes over the agenda for the day.

> Today is a work cycle day, so you all can have time to finish up whatever it is you have left to do. A lot of us are not here, because they're writing AP exams, but the rest of us can get a lot done. All of the gardens need spraying this week, so you have today or Thursday to do it—you are welcome to do it outside of this class time too; just be sure to record it in the Garden folder. The pesticide needs to be applied once each week to ensure healthy plants. I'll be making my way around today to check in with those of you who haven't yet added photos of your work this cycle to your portfolio. Remember, we need to do this to show our funders our work and that we are doing what we say we are doing. Do you all know what I mean by funders?

Some nod, some look blankly, one says no.

"This program is mostly paid for by a grant, not by the school. It's a requirement to demonstrate our work if we'd like to continue to receive funding.

"I also would like to confirm the participation of those who volunteered to sell the rest of our plants and products at the school picnic on Thursday from 5 to 7 p.m. It really helps to have you all there because it highlights these are student products. It also helps to and also promotes interest in the program from the younger students and their parents." He pauses and looks around. The students respond:

"I can go on Thursday."

"I signed up and can make it."

"I think I can do that—will let you know before the end of the day."

"Do you have to be trained to do it?" one student asks.

"I have done it before. I can show you. We use a card reader and cashbox," another responds.

"Terrific, guys, thanks!" the guide says.

> On another note—I want to tell you another reason why selling our products is so important. Last Friday, Peppercorn [a beloved goat] wasn't eating. Don't worry—she is all right but let me tell you what happened. She wasn't eating and I noticed she had a lump in her mouth. She also had a slight fever. I called the farm vet and he was able to see me that night after work—so he checked her out and told us not to worry—thank goodness. But the thing is—we do need to take care of our animals, and we need to call the vet when we are unsure. That costs money. So it's just another reason why we do all these things to make sure we have income coming in—to care for the animals we have, properly.

He finishes, "Okay—let's get started on our work."

One student sets up to pull dried mint off a dried plant to put in tea bags.

Two others start an organizing project for the class in the garden book.

Two more, while eating a snack, try to look and see what they should do. A side conversation about their fruit begins. It is strawberry vs. blackberry. Which side is the top? So that is where the stem goes?

Each student follows their own agenda. There is chatter but not enough to impose on others working in the classroom. Behind me, three students work on choosing photos for their portfolios. It's the end of the year so they are all completing tasks and tying up loose ends. As they do, it prompts thoughts of the future.

"I want to study criminology and psychology. I think eventually I want to become a public defender and help people who really need it. Or maybe an immigration lawyer."

"Really, you don't want to work for a big corporation and make big monies?"

"No, I don't think I could be happy if I saw all the despair of people around me."

"Really? You don't think that Jay-Z is happy?"

"He may be happy with his money on the outside, but you take that away, and he has nothing. Nope. It's not for me," she concludes.

At the other side of the room, the guide is engaged in a conversation with one of the students, who is a senior.

"Are you done with all of your AP exams?"

"Nope, I have one more on Friday, then I am all done. All my senior classes are finished."

"Oh, right, and since everyone is working on exams, classes aren't being held, right?"

"That's right—but I was thinking—could I just do stuff around here? I will have lots of time!"

"Of course! We will have plenty to do!"

"Great."

THE ADOLESCENT STUDENT IN THE 12-18 CLASSROOM

Consider the student entering the third plane of development, identified by Montessori as the ages between 12 and 18, and the span of experiences and growth between younger adolescents (12–15 years old) and older adolescents (15–18 years old). There are certainly physical changes, signs of puberty, and just as notable, changes in students' emotional and social interactions.

> Adolescence is a time when longings awaken with an intensity that many have misunderstood and dismissed as "hormones." The larger questions about meaning, identity, responsibility, and purpose begin to press with an urgency and loneliness we can all remember. Ignored or suppressed, the spiritual forces inside our young turn toxic and explosive. Providing students with opportunities to channel their energy constructively and to explore their mysteries with peers and supportive elders, [can help] young people find balance, integrity, meaning, and connection. (Kessler, 2000, p. xiii)

Neurological changes in the prefrontal cortex are also significant in this second decade of life. Adolescence is "a particularly dynamic period of brain development, second only to infancy. The nature of these changes—in brain structures, functions, and connectivity—allows for a remarkable amount of developmental plasticity unique to this period of life" (National Academies of Sciences, Engineering, and Medicine, 2019, p. 46). When compared to adults, adolescents are less efficient in their ability to plan, to control impulsivity, or to use their working memory and other executive function skills, which can negatively influence learning. Though they crave greater independence (Figure 6.1), they still require scaffolding from the adults in their lives and systems of support embedded in their learning environment (American Montessori Society, n.d.-b). Jenny Anderson and Rebecca Winthrop in a *New York Times* essay (January 2, 2025) pointed out struggles many recent graduates experienced; they

> aren't able to set targets, take initiative, figure things out and deal with setbacks—because in school and at home they were too rarely afforded any agency. Giving kids agency doesn't mean letting them do whatever they want. It doesn't mean lowering expectations, turning education into entertainment or allowing children to choose their own adventure. It means requiring them to identify and pursue some of their own goals, helping them build strategies to reach those goals, assessing their progress and guiding them to course-correct when they fall short.

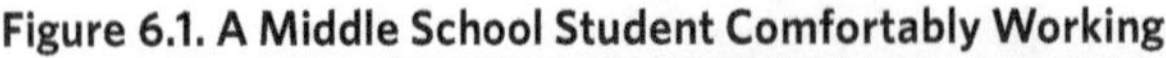

Figure 6.1. A Middle School Student Comfortably Working

Montessori education addresses all of these points.

Montessori curriculum in middle and high school is rigorous. Local standards and state requirements are met and often exceeded as learning shifts from knowledge-building to career application. Students continue to build on foundational math and reading skills, as well as vocabulary and background knowledge across a wide array of topics. They've studied timelines and have a growing understanding of the commonalities and interconnectedness shared among people. Classroom schedules have allowed ample time to build concentration that they now devote to individual interests.

> Activity, depth, breadth, and reflection are woven into this beautiful work. The human story is one that captivates the adolescent and enables us to introduce her to noble figures and diverse personalities of the past. The outrageous and the strong, the weak and the powerful are all poised to teach us about the human condition. (Ludick, 2014, p. 158)

Montessori revisits the concept of education as an aid to life. The adolescent is "a social newborn, now steeped in the mystery of human becoming, now on the cusp of developing her human potential, now recognized as an instrument for peace and change" (Ludick et al., 2009, p. 268). Students are eager to apply all they know and are able to do outside the classroom through self-selected, real-world opportunities. They are curious and creative thinkers, drawn to big-picture ideas. They're compassionate and forgiving; idealists who hold high expectations of themselves and others; often drawn to personal expression through the arts (Ludick, 2014). There's an emphasis on "concrete actions that expose students to a variety of modes of action (justice in all its forms: environmental, gender, education, poverty) . . . their social work needs to have direct, local application and relevance" (Henke, 2017, p. 36). As an example, young adolescents (12–15) may focus on a community issue, or they may choose to shadow a specialist in their area of interest. The older adolescent (15–18) perceives that they are ready to be part of the world. They are ready to take on advocacy roles to address national and global concerns. They've moved beyond "shadowing" a mentor to now applying their skills through internship positions. In the adolescent classroom, curriculum is human-defining, preparing them to be active adults and citizens in today's world.

As we look over the span of development, it's possible to mark students' trajectory. In the first plane of development (0–6 years old), the child worked toward physical autonomy. In the second plane (6–12 years old), they worked toward social competence and intellectual independence. Now, in this third plane, there is a focus on:

- social consciousness, recognizing the different perspectives held by others and learning to work together harmoniously;
- nobility in work, growing engagement and focus, mastery of learning through dialogue and reflection;
- economic independence, micro-economy experiences, engaging in compensated work, and exercising decision-making skills regarding the use of the money they've earned; and
- valorization as witnessed by their optimism, confidence, dignity, self-discipline, initiative, independence, and their ability to work with others, and their commitment to exploring avenues of interest as they self-construct the individual they wish to be (Coe et al., n.d.).

They are no longer children but continue their learning in an interim space situated on the threshold of adulthood.

Student Reflection

I recall a lot of experiences outside of the classroom. Lots of field trips and intercessions, where we had the opportunity to delve into special interests. This felt unique for many reasons, but especially because I had the opportunity to get to know students and teachers in a different way I had might not have otherwise had. For example, we went camping every year. This was a formative time in understanding how to work with others in a much different environment. Planning our meals was probably one of my first experiences in leadership.

—Andi, age 28, Montessori student for 16 years

ENVIRONMENTAL RESPONSE TO DEVELOPMENTAL NEEDS (12–18)

Until this point, *agency* has been used to describe students' freedom and choice in their learning and development. In the adolescent curriculum, there's now a shift toward *valorization,* "Montessori's term for the adolescent's process of becoming a strong and worthy person" (Donahoe et al., 2013, p. 18). In a time where students often feel

> undervalued and misunderstood, the Montessori framework . . . is designed to support the process of valorization, helping them discern their unique strengths, passions, and worth. Montessori middle and high schools champion the adolescent's quest for identity through a rich program of group activities, hands-on projects, and real-world problem solving. (Seldin, 2023)

Through their "work of the mind, hands, and heart," students learn they're useful, they can manage responsibilities and meet challenges—ultimately, they learn that their efforts matter. This is a sensitive period for developing qualities of valorization that align to Duckworth's character development model, including "joy, selflessness, optimism, confidence, dignity, self-discipline, initiative, independence, helpfulness, good judgment, and the ability to work with others" (Donahoe et al., 2013, p. 18).

In conventional education, students are required to complete courses in history and civics that can certainly build knowledge but not necessarily link students personally to this information. The Montessori curriculum nurtures students' civic literacy so they can transform knowledge into active participation in the community. Civic literacy is defined as

> the knowledge of how to actively participate and initiate change in your community and the greater society. It is the foundation by which a democratic society functions . . . as a check and as a means to create avenues for peaceful change." (Stambler, 2013)

Students may opt to take classes at a local college, while others may work with a local nonprofit agency. These activities may require them to learn to navigate the city transportation system, as well as gain confidence in interacting with a variety of adults in settings outside the classroom.

Montessori pointed out the difficulties of standard curricula that were predetermined, scripted, and implemented without input from the students: "It is impossible to fix a priori a detailed program of study and work. We can only give the general plan. This is because a program should only be drawn up gradually under the guidance of experience" (1948/2007, p. 71). Montessori's plan for this age group included Erdkinder schools designed for younger adolescent students (ages 12–15), while Montessori high schools (ages 15–18) and college settings are contemporary interpretations of her work outlined in the appendix of *From*

Childhood to Adolescence (1948/2007). The role of Erdkinders and microeconomics is discussed in the next section.

Student Reflection

I can remember a lot of things! Something that stands out to me was our senior thesis projects, land-based education, and service learning.

—Gabrielle, age 26, Montessori student for 14 years

HOW THE 12-18 MONTESSORI CLASSROOM SUPPORTS PHYSICAL DEVELOPMENT

Students demonstrate an increased capacity for responsibilities requiring greater physical dexterity and coordination through meaningful physical work. Accordingly, the curriculum intentionally continues to refine students' physical skills through the creation of microeconomies and experiential learning opportunities where academic subjects are practiced within them. As an example, writing samples may take the form of business plans students will develop that may include research to secure small business funding. There are often camping and hiking trips (Figure 6.2) that students plan and manage for the entire class, and outdoor classroom environments where students work in gardens that provide for

Figure 6.2. Adolescents Gather After a Hike to Watch the Sunset

the school community. Students physically interact with the local permaculture, as we saw in the adolescent vignette, preparing and tending a garden, raising chickens or tilapia for consumption. In some schools, microeconomies may include running a store where eggs, produce, bakery items, and handcrafted materials are made available to the community. All of these experiences require physical engagement as a necessary component of learning.

Though microeconomies is the term most popularly used in Montessori programs today, Montessori actually referred to this work as *production and exchange* (1948/2007). She referred to this group of students as *Erdkinder*—children of the earth. Historically, these classrooms were often situated in rural settings. Students maintained farms and managed place-based microeconomies producing and managing the sale of their efforts. For these students, Montessori believed their work was

> an introduction both to nature and to civilization, [giving them] a limitless field for scientific and historic studies. If the produce can be used commercially this brings in the fundamental mechanism of society, that of production and exchange, on which economic life is based. This means that there is an opportunity to learn both academically and through actual experience what are the elements of social life. We have called these children the "Erdkinder" because they are learning about civilization through its origin in agriculture. They are the "land-children." (1948/2007, p. 68)

For today's students, the essence of this learning model continues to support their ability to value both *production* and *exchange* of goods. Some microeconomy programs may still take place in farming communities where students "work and live together in a rural setting developing social independence, economic and business skills" (Brunold-Conesa, 2025). Other adolescent programs retain the rigor of learning by offering alternative experiences, including

> honors-based or college level academics, elective courses in creative expression, humanities, and STEM areas, year-long senior projects where students explore individual interests through interdisciplinary research, cultural exchange and trips abroad to build intercultural awareness and global citizenship, off-campus service learning, internships, environmental stewardship, and peace education. (Brunold-Conesa, 2025)

The Montessori adolescent curriculum focuses on "creating something, transforming raw materials into useful products, providing a service that is of actual need in the wider community . . . adolescents need the opportunity to work with their hands, whether tending the garden, welding a piece of sculpture, or plating gourmet meals to produce something of value from start to finish. There is satisfaction in the process of creation but also in seeing that item be valued enough by another person to be exchanged for money" (Dowell, n.d.). Where the adolescent program is located and which microeconomy is led by the students are secondary considerations. What is most important is that the adolescent student feels purpose in their work, and that they are engaged in activities that have meaning and impact their community.

HOW THE 12-18 MONTESSORI CLASSROOM SUPPORTS COGNITIVE DEVELOPMENT

Language continues to play a significant role in the Montessori curriculum. Adolescents are on the precipice of adulthood, and language reflects their real-life experiences, intellectual development, and the skills needed to define their place in the world. Without words, without expressive language, humans struggle to be active participants in a community or be successful in human relationships. Table 6.1 offers an overview of the language lessons embedded in the Montessori adolescent curriculum.

Since high-level discourse is a key element of the adolescent classroom, language—both the vocabulary and concepts known to students (receptive language) and how one shares their thoughts, ideas, and knowledge (expressive language)—are essential skills. Rather than a pedagogy of telling (Sizer, 1985), where teachers deliver content to students via lecture, educators in Montessori adolescent classrooms promote a pedagogy of dialogue. The adult's role is one of facilitator using an inquiry model. Students share their thinking prior to the adult sharing their own. Open-ended questions are asked to engage students in dialogue. Novel materials are offered to encourage discussion. The guide liberally uses wait time, trusting in the dialogic process with their students (Nelson, 2023). Students learn to consider diverse perspectives, connect ideas, and evaluate conclusions and sources. Research has shown that these practices contribute to students' higher-order thinking, their ability to think more critically, and expand their sociocultural mindsets, while also learning to collaborate (Nelson, 2023, p. 63). Ultimately, the guide and students co-construct knowledge.

Table 6.1. Language Developed in the Montessori Adolescent Classroom

- The language of grace and courtesy
- The language of place, the language of community/common ground
- The language of civility and citizenship
- The interactive language of academia as it connects to all of the disciplines (history, science, mathematics, philosophy, etc.)
- The language of discourse and debate
- The language of politics, of analysis, of diplomacy
- The language of theology, philosophy, spirituality
- The language of business, economics, government
- The language that honors human sexuality and human love
- The language of gesture and facial expression
- The language of the arts: visual, dramatic, musical, craft, poetry
- The language of rhetoric, propaganda
- The language of technology, the media
- The powerful language of the natural world
- And, so importantly, the language of silence

Source: Ludick et al., 2009, pp. 269–270.

Of the many dialogic practices, four instructional strategies are frequently observed in Montessori classrooms: literature circles, modeling instruction, Socratic seminars, and the Harkness method. Literature circles reflect dialogue around a shared reading. Students learn to listen, to take turns, and to support their comments using text references. Modeling instruction supports students' understanding of science by asking them to make predictions and develop models that describe a science lesson. Socratic seminars are dialogues around an area of study that allow students to co-construct meaning. There is often a shared text that students annotate prior to the discussion. Students are assigned roles. Adults may lead these discussions initially, but once students are familiar with the protocols, they'll facilitate discussions. And the Harkness model was designed to create a more democratic learning environment. A group gathers at a table to engage in dialogue with the teacher, offering context or clarification, and a student taking the lead as the moderator. Graph paper is used to map and then analyze student talk time (Nelson, 2023).

Technology can now be a partner in these dialogic experiences. Equity Maps is a subscription-free app that builds on the Harkness model by tracking who is speaking as well as the number of times and amount of time each person spoke, while also creating a visual conversation map illustrating the flow of the discussion (Figure 6.3). It's a novel tool that allows users to use an iPad to record group

Figure 6.3. Equity Map

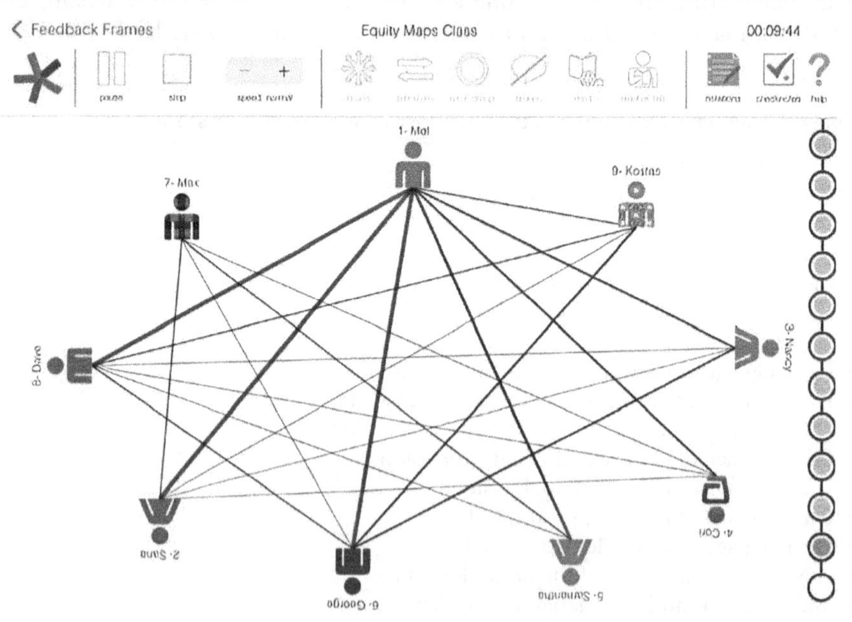

discussions to "track teacher talk, the use of media, silence, small group work, pair-share, and chaos (capturing more than one simultaneous conversation)" (Nelson, 2023, p. 25). Data are currently only collected by the user, and results offer students and educators immediate feedback using snapshots of individual and group dynamics. Equity Maps also consider gender distributions to identify the frequency of student contributions to group discussion. The tool also tracks the types of contributions made by each person (e.g., did they ask a clarifying question, make a connection to a personal experience, pose a thought-provoking question, etc.). The tool makes learning visible to all participants, helps to raise awareness around teacher talk, and promotes inclusive learning environments, thus ensuring that all voices are heard. It also serves as a dialogic partner, supporting students' metacognition of their own speaking and listening practices—a life skill that will serve them well beyond their time in the classroom.

STUDENT REFLECTION

In elementary and middle school, students gain a lot of background knowledge and are increasingly able to control their education. As they begin to understand what they are interested in, they are given the agency to expand on that knowledge. Reports in elementary and papers in UE [Upper Elementary] and middle school are the examples I'm thinking of. When I was in middle school, I had learned enough about science to know I was interested in genetics, and my sister had a genetic disability, so I wrote a paper on my sister's disability, which launched my passion for health science.

Montessori has always met me where I'm at and helped me excel. When I was 4 I was ready to learn to read, so I was given that opportunity. In fifth grade I was ready for Algebra I, so I was put in the class and really enjoyed it. Every student is in a different place, and Montessori does an excellent job at addressing each child's specific needs. This culture extends beyond education.

—Sarah, age 20, Montessori student for 12 years

As stated earlier, the curriculum aligns to standards and meets educational requirements specific to the state where it's located. Some schools have a clear scope and sequence outlining the curriculum and its alignment to standards. Others will meet these same objectives but will use cover sheets or a framework for each unit of study. Unlike a syllabus, a cover sheet is not prepopulated with assignments and activities. Instead, broad themes are suggested for study, and students work with their guide to co-construct how these topics will be explored and evaluated over the next several weeks. There is a brief narrative at the top of the cover sheet that uses language to inspire wonder and excitement about an upcoming study. There are guiding questions, learning objectives, and a diverse number of ways students determine how they will demonstrate their learning.

In one classroom, students were introduced to a broad theme of Peace, Love, and Justice. From late January to the end of March, students decided to study the Civil War and the Reconstruction period; they elected to study historical connections to the legacy of slavery in their community, they selected readings on these topics, and they planned discussions about ethics in research and genetics. There were also planned sessions related to physical health and well-being, and computer and math skills (quadratic equations). They also chose to write comparative essays of classic stories and their contemporary interpretations.

During that unit of study, some lessons were delivered seminar style, where relevant vocabulary was introduced during mini-lessons. In the above example, history and slavery were explored through students' reading of *James* (Everett, 2024). As a shared text, group discussions tackled larger questions about identity, equity, purpose, and ethics, demonstrating how literature helps students become "enthralled with the ideas, feelings, and language of literature itself . . . [offering] vicarious entry into worlds outside their direct experience" (Suhor, 1998). The use of Socratic discussions supported students' ability to understand their own perspectives, as well as the views of others, especially those who did not align to their own thinking. And they practiced expressive language skills, supporting their thinking with content learned in their studies. All of these are viable skills needed to be adults ready to participate in society beyond the classroom.

HOW THE 12–18 MONTESSORI CLASSROOM SUPPORTS CHARACTER DEVELOPMENT—JUDGMENT AND PROACTIVITY

Judgment skills and proactivity are two character traits nurtured in adolescent Montessori classrooms. Proactive individuals, according to Duckworth (n.d.-g),

> don't accept the world as it is or wait for direction from others to initiate change. Instead, they take matters into their own hands, acting to make the world better for themselves and others. They speak truth to power, take charge to solve problems, and champion new ideas.

Judgment is the process of recognizing our internal biases so we may review and identify the best possible answer (Duckworth, n.d.-h). Whether engaging in small business projects or managing difficult discussions in classroom council meetings, adolescent students use their judgment and proactivity skills daily in the Montessori classroom.

Designing a small business venture requires the ability to make decisions, including pricing materials, determining who will need to be part of the team to ensure the project's success, and developing a reasonable timeline. Some student projects are successful, others less so. Mistakes are understood to be part of the learning process. If a project fails, it is not the end of the endeavor; rather, it is an opportunity to think deeply through the project and determine any needed revisions to successfully execute the plan.

And when tensions arise in the classroom, students will initiate and lead council meetings informed by guidelines they created at the beginning of the year. Students learn to share and respectfully listen and respond to the perspectives of others. Again, judgments are discussed thoroughly, with lots of opportunities to discuss values and time to process the discussion. In each of these scenarios, adults are always available to offer support when needed. But it's the student who learns about duty and responsibility to themselves and others.

Many adolescent (and some Upper Elementary) programs participate in the Montessori Model United Nations (MMUN). In its early days, Montessori challenged UNESCO to involve children in peace-building activities. Her words sparked the creation of the MMUN, turning her vision into an opportunity for young people to have a voice in global conversations. Through research, collaboration, and diplomacy experiences, MMUN transforms students from knowledge seekers to agents of change as they learn about the world and their capacity to improve it.

Unlike traditional Model UN programs—which often emphasize competition, rapid debate, and performance—MMUN is intentionally designed to reflect Montessori developmental principles and values. Table 6.2 outlines differences in the models. MMUN offers students online diplomatic practice sessions with peers from around the world, building confidence and fluency in the UN's Rules of Procedure while deepening cultural understanding. There are social meetups

Table 6.2. Comparison Chart: Model UN Program and Montessori Model UN

Traditional Model UN	Montessori Model UN (MMUN)
Competitive and award-based	Collaborative and consensus-based
Focus on debate and winning	Focus on listening, empathy, and shared solutions
Suited to high school or university students	Designed for Upper Elementary and adolescents (ages 9–15)
Fast-paced, adult-modeled	Developmentally appropriate and reflective
Performance-driven	Process-oriented and student-led
Limited attention to student agency	Deep respect for the moral voice of youth
Preparation is isolated and academic	Includes global community-building and real-world preparation

to help students form friendships, learn about each other's cultures, and experience what it means to live in a global community. MMUN then culminates at the MMUN Conference held online and in person in New York, Rome, and Bangkok in conjunction with the United Nations. Here students step into the role of UN Ambassador, engaging in high-level dialogue and proposing real-world solutions (J. Cunningham, personal communication, July 20, 2025).

When supporting students' character development, it's important to note the growing demands they face in an ever-changing landscape. Three recent reports share similar themes and recommendations that hold particular significance for those who work with adolescents: *The Human Flourishing Study* (2025), Ellen Galinsky's (2024) research from *The Breakthrough Years*, and the parting prescription written by then U.S. Surgeon General Dr. Vivek Murthy (2025). Each carries a clarion call related to the experience of belonging, "a fundamental human need—the feeling of deep connection with social groups, physical places, and individual and collective experiences" (Murthy, 2025, p. 7).

First, according to the study conducted by Gallup (2025), flourishing is a measurement of an individual's well-being within the context of their community and local environment. The study investigated the mediating factors that contribute to a well-lived life. More than measuring a single indicator such as happiness, the study aimed to understand human flourishing as a "state of complete physical, social, emotional, cognitive, volitional and spiritual wellbeing" (Gallup, 2025, p. 4). Over 200,000 participants from 22 countries completed the survey, with outcomes highlighting a warning about our young people. They pointed to

> evidence of a mental health crisis and increase in loneliness in the U.S. that has disproportionately affected young adults . . . [T]o improve the well-being of our young people [they recommended], comprehensive mental health services, supporting education and meaningful employment, and strengthening [the] social fabric for young people." (Chen et al., 2022, pp. 1046–47).

Ellen Galinsky (2024), in her book *The Breakthrough Years: A New Scientific Framework for Raising Thriving Teens*, shared outcomes of a survey she conducted with over 1,600 adolescents between the ages of 9 and 18 years old and their parents. These young people noted that their need for belonging was primarily met by family (88%), followed by friends (76%) and out-of-school activities: sports, band, clubs (66%), while the need for belonging was least met in schools (60%) or online (56%). When adolescents experienced a sense of belonging, their engagement at school increased, they had a more positive outlook on the future, and they experienced less stress and fewer negative emotions. These survey results are compelling reminders that creating learning environments and human exchanges that reflect the particular needs of adolescents is imperative to their well-being.

And in his final message as U.S. Surgeon General to the American public, Vivek Murthy (2025) offered a prescription in response to his study addressing the profound influence of isolation and loneliness experienced by so many in our country. Studies linked our society's growing social disconnection, depression, cognitive decline, growing anxiety, and other negative health concerns. These outcomes could be reversed with an increased focus on relationships, service, and purpose. This became his prescription, a triad of fulfillment: relationships, service, and purpose, core elements of community, combined with the core virtue of love, to create an ecosystem of meaning and belonging (Murthy, 2025).

Murthy's recommendations deeply align to Montessori adolescent education as students engage in developing healthy relationships with peers and adults every day, both inside and outside the classroom. Students in adolescent classrooms have access to adult mentors who serve as models of civility. Results from both Galinsky (2024) and Gallup (2024) highlighted that when young adults feel appreciated for who they are, supportive relationships can serve as a buffer to stress, as well as a powerful source of joy.

Later in this chapter, additional reflections from the survey conducted with Montessori alumni echo similar expressions of their need to feel appreciated, and to be known for individual strengths and interests. The alumni also recognized the value of their community service activities and how they led to a greater sense of purpose felt well beyond the classroom.

THE ROLE OF THE ADULT IN THE 12–18 CLASSROOM

The Association Montessori Internationale (AMI) requires that adults working with students from 12 to 18 years of age be responsive to their students' "special stage of life, on the threshold of adulthood" (12–18, n.d.-e). Educators create classroom environments that

> reflect all aspects of adult life and provide opportunities, not only to pursue academic interests but also participate in real adult practical work in a social setting as close to a real society as possible. Through experiences of everyday life and its responsibilities, the adolescents will practice what it takes to become a contributing member of a wider society.
>
> This experience includes an initiation into economics and an understanding of its importance for everyday life. Another important aspect of the environment is that it should put the adolescents in close contact with nature in order to instill an appreciation and understanding of the responsibility of the planet on which we live and are a part of. (AMI, 12–18, n.d.-e)

Similarly, the American Montessori Society's School Accreditation Standards (2023) require adolescent educators (Secondary I, 12–14/15 and Secondary II, 14/15–18) to facilitate a curriculum that includes the core curriculum areas of Math, Language Arts, Social Studies, Science, Additional/World Language, and Creative Arts, the Secondary curriculum, [and also] includes opportunities for community service, career exploration, economic awareness, technology, peace, social justice, and cosmic education, physical education, outdoor education, and field studies.

The curriculum prepares students for postsecondary education or careers through self-construction, extensive self-reflection, identity development, self-advocacy, and opportunities for leadership and personal responsibility. Personality integration and stewardship of the earth and humanity are crucial elements of the curriculum. Students' independent decision-making, problem-solving, community-building, and application of learning indicate successful implementation of the curriculum. (AMS Standard 3.3.4, p. 4)

Adolescent Montessori educators are specialists in a given field. They enter Montessori training with a degree in a subject area (e.g., history, math, science). Their training offers the philosophical layer demonstrating developmentally appropriate ways to share their knowledge with students. This is different from Montessori educators who work with younger children—they are considered generalists; using a curriculum made up of lessons that were presented to them, they studied, practiced, and made them their own in their training years.

Adolescent guides can pivot to instructional approaches based on their students' developmental needs. As an example, Michael Waski (2017), a math teacher in a Montessori high school in Cleveland, Ohio, reflected on the characteristics of young adolescents compared to those of older adolescents. He described differences in students' reactions when offered a "brain teaser" to work through a mathematical problem. When working with his younger students, he found that there's

> an immediate frenzy of activity: people throwing out ideas and opinions, lots of discussion . . . and the students will definitely be engaged with the material in a visible way. In the end, there may be some students who are at different levels of understanding and so after the group work they will have some individual work where they can process their own thoughts and ideas and consolidate their understanding wherever they may be. (p. 7)

However, when working with the older adolescents, he described their response as an initial period of silence, a longer pause (Figure 6.4). Waski (2017) noted that these students

> will start to do work on their own before sharing their ideas. This is certainly not because they are afraid to be wrong in front of their peers . . . Instead there is a different type of processing that is happening. These students need solitary time first,

Figure 6.4. Middle School Students Collaborating

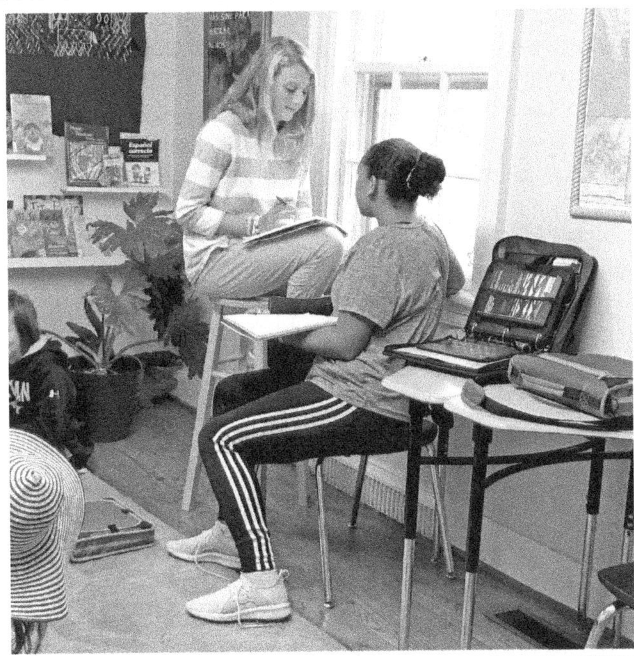

> and then they are more than happy to, and indeed need to come together in groups to share where they are in their thinking, to seek help, and to collaborate. (p. 7)

Educators must be well versed in human development. Just as teachers are prepared to offer developmentally appropriate content based on a student's readiness and interests, "it is essential that we match our methodology with the psychology of the adolescent and as this changes throughout adolescence, so should our approach" (Waski, 2017, p. 9) to our work with students.

Teaching is complex, often requiring persistence from both the educator and their students. To foster independence, educators create classrooms where answers require more than an adult's input. Students implement their research skills. Systems are in place where cover sheets or a syllabus offer readings and links for students to further explore study topics. Using these skills helps students

> flourish into responsible, empathetic, and confident adults, [where] Montessori middle and high schools serve as catalysts in this transformative journey. By valorizing each student, they lay the foundation for lifelong success, ensuring our children are prepared for both the academic rigors of university and the broader challenges of life. (Seldin, 2023)

STUDENT REFLECTION

My JH/HS Montessori experience shaped who I am as a person today. My teachers and peers helped guide me through adolescence in a way that made me feel like I could take risks (academically, personally) but still felt safe. My teachers always recognized when I needed more challenging work academically and provided ways for me to stay engaged with material. As a kid who was very shy and socially anxious, I can't imagine a better place for me during these years. Being able to stay with a small cohort of students for multiple years helped me build relationships I wouldn't have been able to otherwise. The collaborative learning environment forced me to speak to others and gain important social skills. I don't remember much about materials in the classroom, but learning about forces of nature by doing trapeze, or about outdoor survival skills while actually surviving outside is pretty powerful.

—Elena, age 29, Montessori student for 7 years

STUDENT REFLECTION

Being a part of a farm-based Montessori middle school gave me an understanding of economics, cooking, and manual labor skills. My high school Montessori experience really instilled notions of community, engagement, high-level education, and a reasonable level of silliness throughout!

—Eddie, age 22, Montessori student for 15 years

MONTESSORI ALUMNI REFLECTIONS

The previous chapters outlined elements of Montessori education using a developmental continuum lens. Following children from infancy through adolescence, they have provided reflections with rich descriptions of child and adult interactions, materials and activities typically available in classroom settings, and the role of the educator.

To close out the review of Montessori classrooms, we return to Adele Diamond's request for researchers to gather direct feedback from individuals who have firsthand experience of a program. In response to this request, we developed an online survey requesting Montessori alumni to share their retrospective reflections of their classroom experience, as well as insight related to their role as students beyond high school and their current role in the workforce. We have shared brief snippets and summaries from the many in-depth responses received from survey participants. Insight from current and previous students can offer

Montessori school administrators and district personnel data to inform evaluation and continuous improvement plans. Future research in Montessori education should also consider students as a rich qualitative source of data to enhance their quantitative results.

More than 85 participants responded to the online survey. They ranged in age from 18 to 78 years old, and lived across the United States (CO, NH, IL, NC, GA, MI, WA, CT, OR, AZ, TX, NY, FL, RI, CA, VA, OH, MA, WA, KS, IN, TN, MT, WI), as well as in Canada, Belgium, and Japan. Here's a summary of their responses.

Reflections: Being a student in a Montessori classroom. Many respondents shared memories of being students in 3–6 and 6–12 Montessori classrooms. Given the preponderance of classrooms available at these age levels, the results make sense. Almost all responses were positive, though a few respondents recalled instances of feeling excluded or spoke of difficulties being in classrooms where teachers were not prepared to meet the needs of dual-language learners. Currently, there are some Montessori schools in larger urban districts that lead dual-language programs, although more are certainly needed so that all children can communicate in multiple languages in preparation for their role as global citizens.

Notably, many respondents shared memories related to friendship, classrooms that felt like home, and feelings of safety, along with opportunities to self-select work and stay engaged with content for extended periods of time. Some recalled the names of certain Montessori materials, while most gave vivid descriptions of how they recalled using the materials. Regardless of when the memory took place—some dated back 30 years or more!—there were strong similarities across positive responses with little variation based on where in the world the alumni had attended Montessori schools.

Reflections: Being a student beyond the Montessori classroom. About a third of the respondents self-identified as students working on undergraduate or graduate degrees in business, geography, American studies, education, computer science, bioengineering, urban studies and ethnicity, race and migration, advanced language certificate in French, mechanical engineering, film, classics, speech pathology, and social work, as well as doctoral students studying experimental psychology and medicine. When asked if they believed being enrolled in Montessori classrooms influenced their work as college students, an overwhelming 100% of respondents expressed their belief that there was a positive influence on their learning beyond the Montessori classroom.

Reflections: The influence of Montessori education as a working professional. Of the participants who identified as working professionals, 97% believed that their experience in Montessori classrooms influenced their current roles as working professionals. They held positions as software engineers, data visualization analysts in the criminal justice field, trust and estate planning in banking, risk management, baristas, librarians, mental health clinicians, speech language pathologists, clinical social workers, therapists, lawyers, and researchers. Some described volunteering in their communities, serving in the military, or creating their own businesses, and some were now educators who returned to teach in Montessori classrooms or who prepared future Montessori educators!

Responses described beliefs about independence and ability to work at their own pace without the need to make comparisons to colleagues. Respondents described themselves as communicators, collaborators, and problem-solvers. They were flexible thinkers, hard-working, leaders in their field, and worked well with colleagues who were diverse in age and culture. Here are some additional comments:

1. As a social worker, social justice is paramount to the profession, that started at Montessori. I also think on a base level, Montessori informed my belief that every single person is capable of learning, changing, and growing when given access to tools, and the simple belief from someone that they CAN. Rachel—Michigan
2. As a software engineer, self-directed problem-solving is a primary responsibility of my role and I believe my Montessori experience set me up well for these tasks. Jonathan—New Hampshire
3. This is difficult to divorce as I work within Montessori settings. However, I think the biggest impact is that I expect my work to bring me joy and be joyful. When I talk to peers who did not have a Montessori background, even those who attended the same liberal arts college as me, there seems to be an expectation that work should feel difficult and that it is something to put up with in return for money. I think my childhood Montessori education empowered me to feel equipped to tackle any new experience I might wish to try my hand at. Whether it be building a new business or learning a new technical skill, I am at ease trying and failing and trying again. Zil—Oregon
4. Yes, in many ways. Especially in high school, we were taught how to navigate the city in which we lived and to immerse ourselves in institutions and facilities. We traveled all over, almost a school without walls. The other thing is that I find myself tending to think outside of the box and exploring multiple solutions. In general, it also led me to want to de-escalate conflict and while I'm as human as anyone else, I tended to want to . . . look for common ground whenever possible. Tim—Florida
5. I can conceptualize new initiatives faster than my peers. Additionally, I can adapt to changes quicker than most. I can perform mental math and articulate outcomes to different audience levels clearly. Markus—Illinois

On a final note, responses from Montessori alumni can also help to predict trends in future workforce requirements. In an ever-evolving employment landscape, the World Economic Forum (2025) gathered survey data from over 1,000 employers to better understand employment trends. The industry leaders represented over 14 million workers globally, and results of the global survey offered

Table 6.3. Core Skills for the 2025–2030 Workforce

Cognitive Skills	Self-Efficacy
• Analytical thinking • Creative thinking • Systems thinking • Multilingualism • Reading, writing, and mathematics	• Resilience, flexibility, and agility • Motivation and self-awareness • Curiosity and lifelong learning • Dependability and attention to detail
Working With Others	**Technology Skills**
• Leadership and social influence • Empathy and active listening • Teaching and mentoring	• Technological literacy • AI and big data • Networks and cybersecurity • Design and user experience • Programming
Management Skills	**Engagement Skills**
• Talent management • Resource management and operations • Quality control	• Service orientation and customer service • Marketing and media
Ethics	**Physical Abilities**
• Environmental stewardship • Global citizenship	• Manual dexterity, endurance, and precision • Sensory-processing abilities

Source: World Economic Forum (2025); adapted from Future of Jobs Survey, p. 35.

predictive insights into the required core skills needed by the workforce over the next 5 years. Table 6.3, Core Skills for the 2025–2030 Workforce, highlights trends in eight key areas: cognitive skills, self-efficacy, working with others, technology skills, management skills, engagement skills, ethics, and physical abilities. These skills are intentionally embedded within the Montessori curriculum for students to master in the classroom, prior to entering the workforce.

Thus far, we have explored Montessori classrooms from infancy through adolescence. The next chapter will expand the view beyond the Montessori school to include the many organizations that uphold Montessori education globally.

CHAPTER 7

Expanding Our View: The Montessori Ecosystem

Chapters 3 through 6 provided an overview of Montessori education, highlighting its pedagogy and principles, supported by best practices currently recognized in education. Each chapter focused on multi-age classrooms, describing the materials, students' developmental needs, and instructional approaches used by educators to support all students, as well as reflections from Montessori alumni. These interactions align with Bronfenbrenner's ecological model (1979), where the child is the innermost sphere (the microsystem), along with the earliest influences from family members and caregivers. When the child and family become engaged in Montessori education, the sphere then widens to include the interactions between home and school (mesosystem).

In this chapter, the reader's view is extended beyond the classroom to consider the multifaceted system needed to sustain Montessori education in both the independent and public sectors in Bronfenbrenner's exosystem. It's important to recognize that Montessori classrooms do not exist as stand-alone entities; rather, they are situated within an ecosystem of programming. Figure 7.1 highlights the exosystem, or constellation of organizations that are foundational to the sustainability, growth, and access to Montessori education for families.

The Montessori constellation includes national and international affiliations that serve as professional development and membership hubs for educators, administrators, and other school personnel. It also includes teacher preparation programs, research collectives, and organizations that design and build Montessori materials. There are programs to monitor quality and validate teacher education programs and schools to ensure that a standard of excellence that aligns to Montessori principles is upheld. There are state and national organizations that focus on advocacy efforts ranging from teacher licensure to recognition of the Montessori curriculum through individual state departments of education. Montessori organizations are also devoted to efforts to increase access across the human continuum, focused on growth in public school and out-of-school time opportunities—as well as alternative applications of the Montessori pedagogy such as youth sports, elder care, and programming that supports older adults living with dementia.

Figure 7.1. Montessori Constellation—Exosystems

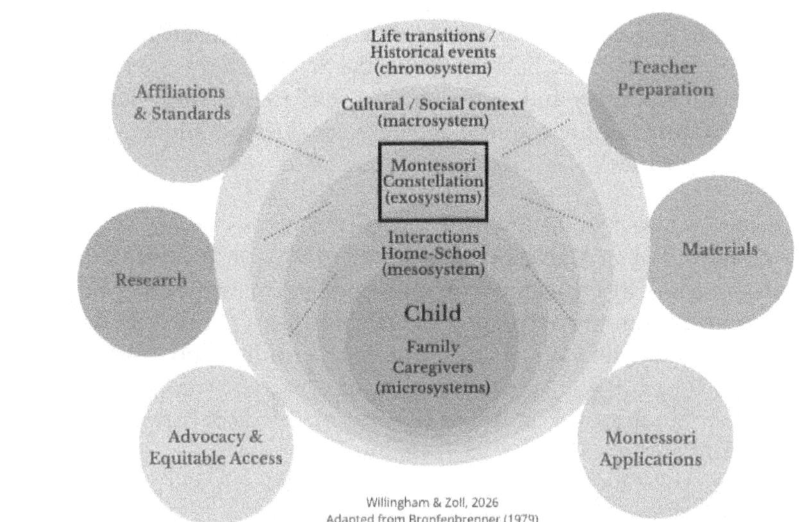

This ever-growing framework of state, national, and international organizations (of which some are listed below) includes brief annotations curated through analysis of publicly available information to define this bright constellation of Montessori education. A listing of current websites is available in the Appendix. Collectively, these organizations allow educators and children to thrive in their educational settings. Although the list is not exhaustive, it does help orient those new to Montessori education by providing some references to further explore within the broader world of Montessori education.

Montessori Affiliations and Standards are the national and international organizations that retain membership, often aligned to an educators' training. They host conferences, while also supporting research and advocacy efforts. The two oldest entities serve constituents globally—the Association Montessori Internationale (AMI) and the American Montessori Society (AMS). Additional organizations include the International Montessori Council (IMC) and Montessori Education Programs International (MEPI), among others. Many of these organizations also lead accreditation or recognition processes for partnering schools that meet programmatic standards. Together, they support private, public, and charter Montessori schools through professional development, conferences, coaching, and other activities to support teachers and school administrators.

Teacher Education Programs (TEPs) are Montessori training programs situated in university and independent settings. Their programs are implemented via hybrid and residency-based delivery methods. Their purpose is to train educators to teach using the Montessori pedagogy across specific age groups: 0–3, 3–6, 6–12, and 12–18. Some TEPs offer certification in inclusive education for children with identified learning and behavioral needs, while others offer Montessori-informed care for the aging and dementia care. TEPs associated with institutions of higher education offer programs at the undergraduate, graduate, and doctoral levels. Examples include

- University-Based TEPs: Loyola University, Sarasota University, Hartford University, Xavier University, University of Wisconsin-River Falls
- Independent TEPs: Cincinnati Montessori Secondary Teacher Education (CMStep), Montessori Training Center Northeast (MTCNE), Montessori Institute—New England, Montessori Teacher Education Institute of Atlanta
- Inclusive Montessori Education: Montessori Medical Partnerships for Inclusion, Shelton Montessori Training
- Montessori Aging and Elder Care: Montessori for Aging and Dementia, Montessori for Dementia, Disability, and Ageing

To assure program quality, many teacher education programs have earned accreditation from the Montessori Accreditation Council for Teacher Education (MACTE). MACTE has been recognized as an accreditation body by the U.S. Department of Education since 1995.

Montessori Materials are the visible tools in the classroom environment modeled by trained educators. Nienhuis, founded in 1929 through a collaboration with Dr. Montessori to develop her novel materials, is the largest distributor of Montessori materials globally. Montessori Services offers an array of materials across the curriculum, with a particular focus on Practical Life manipulatives. Learning Sunshine is a resource for books related to Montessori and special education. Maitri Learning offers research-based educational materials to support language and literacy-rich classrooms and organizations that support children's multilingual learning. This is a mere sampling of the many organizations offering Montessori resources. Additional organizations can be accessed through attendance at regional and national Montessori conferences.

Montessori Research is a growing area of study. The American Montessori Society hosts the AMS Research Committee, the American Montessori Society Archive housed at the University of Connecticut, the *Journal of Montessori Research*, and a compendium of research articles and resources available on their website. The Association Montessori Internationale also hosts a virtual resource library and historical publications archived in the Netherlands. Additional publications exist through the archived NAMTA Journals (North American Montessori Teachers Association), also managed by the Association Montessori Internationale.

Other research entities include the Montessori Science Program located at the University of Virginia. Researchers there have recently completed a literature review organized across a host of educational topics (e.g., assessment, mixed-age classrooms, student autonomy and choice, etc.). There are also research studies conducted by the Center for Montessori Studies (University of Hartford), as well as the Montessori Research Collective.

Montessori Advocacy and Equitable Access are led by many of the organizations listed previously in the Affiliations section. Montessori Public Policy Institute (MPPI) is a joint collaboration between AMS and AMI-USA, serving as a coordinated voice in public policy initiatives. Their work has led to many state departments of education recognizing Montessori teaching credentials and successfully including Montessori language (reading/ELA) materials as recognized curriculum meeting science of reading legislation. One project, led by the Khalsa Montessori School (AZ) in collaboration with MPPI and NCMPS (see Brown et al., 2024), documents the power of collaboration to initiate change and greater access of Montessori education in publicly funded settings.

The National Center for Montessori in the Public Sector (NCMPS) works with practitioners and school personnel from primary through adolescent classrooms (teachers, coaches, school leaders, district coordinators and leaders, charter authorizers), policymakers, researchers, parents, and advocates, serving as a hub for all things public Montessori. Similar work is also led by AMS, AMI, and IMC to meet the needs of their constituents. And these organizations host conferences and other professional development opportunities to address the particular needs of Montessori public and charter schools.

Montessori on Wheels (MoW) partners with schools and families to create accessible Montessori experiences that redefine learning and that can and should happen in any location. Funding from private foundations have been invested in creating tuition-free, Montessori-inspired early childhood programs that take place in a beautifully designed school bus. They've also developed programming to build school leadership through an innovative teacher-leader model.

Additional Montessori Applications create responsive programming that remains aligned to Montessori principles. As an example, there are growing efforts to promote adult well-being. Katie Keller Wood's book, *Alignment: A Montessori Approach to Reimagining Work-Life Balance* (2025), supports holistic living for adults. Montessori Sports integrates movement into the Montessori curriculum. Montessori-Orff Music offers training to bring rhythm and lyrics into classrooms at all levels as a tool for equity and connection. For older students, Montessori Model United Nations, as previously described, offers programs for Upper Elementary and adolescent students in various locations around the world, including Rome, New York, and Bangkok. And several organizations offer research and training related to elder care and supporting individuals identified with dementia using a Montessori approach to setting up living environments and planning intentional activities and interactions between older adults and their caregivers.

Currently, education in the United States is undergoing a seismic transition. However, impacts from funding loss and institutional dismantlement may be less devastating for the Montessori field, particularly if school operations have not been dependent on state or federal funding. The Ecosystem of Montessori Education is a self-regulating system constructed over the last century. Rather than electing to morph a humanistic and developmentally centered pedagogy to meet expectations set by an antiquated industrial education model, the Montessori community has remained true to its foundational beliefs. One strength of this self-sustaining system is its belief in its educators. Since there is an agreed-upon curriculum and instructional approach that's implemented across all age groups, Montessori educators experience autonomy in the classroom. Many independent Montessori schools are unencumbered by the growing number of political mandates and shifts in curriculum selections that influence instruction in publicly funded schools. Autonomy in teaching and the opportunity to nurture one's instructional practice to mastery is critical in Montessori environments. Though this structure is critical to any teaching practice, support has been eroding in conventional education in preceding decades.

As the nation has shifted educational priorities in reading instruction, implemented underfunded instructional approaches, and mandated policies dictated under federal education policies from No Child Left Behind, Race to the Top, and the Every Student Succeeds Act, the field of Montessori education has remained steadfast in its work with students. Montessori educators, school administrators, teacher preparation faculty, and a diverse array of leadership continue to uphold and build upon the pedagogy developed by Montessori, a comprehensive model that collectively works to support the child. One of the greatest strengths of Montessori education may be its perpetual drive to hold the child at the epicenter. The child is ground zero. And everything else has been built around that center.

CLOSING AND NEXT STEPS IN MONTESSORI EDUCATION

The Montessori pedagogy is not a perfect form of education, but the approaches to teaching and learning outlined in this book can improve individualized instruction that responds to the developmental needs all children. As a field, the Montessori community could benefit from stronger connections between what happens in classrooms and educational research. Dr. Montessori would have continued her scientific examination of the pedagogy—no less should be considered of current Montessori educators. Instructional approaches proven in conventional classrooms that also align with Montessori principles should be considered for use in Montessori classrooms, especially those that better meet the needs of students. And the inverse holds true as well: Montessori educators can share their work with the greater field of education. There are similarities between best practices implemented in conventional and Montessori classrooms. One educator may use the I Do-We Do-You Do instructional strategy, while the other uses the

3-period lesson. Although the approaches are quite similar, it's often a language issue that keeps one educator from understanding the other. Increased visibility of Montessori education through publications, partnerships with researchers, and presentations at regional and national conferences will help to build understanding for those who outside the Montessori constellation.

As students are prepared to serve as global citizens, additional attention is needed to meet the needs of multilingual learners while also broadening the scope of the curriculum to teach multiple languages simultaneously to all children. In one of her last speeches, Montessori (1949/1964) reiterated her grand vision of education as a path to peace. Her speech offered hope in our future as a human collective. When children's needs are met (physical, cognitive, and character development), a new humanity will arise. We'll collectively uphold human values, and each individual will

> rebel against the thought that contradictory moral principles can exist within him simultaneously, nor can he accept being simultaneously the supporter of two kinds of justice, one that protects life, the other that destroys it; nor can he allow himself to cultivate in his heart both love and hate; nor can he tolerate two disciplines, one that aims to gather human energies together for constructive purposes and the other that gathers the same energy for the destruction of what has been built. (p. 11)

These are lofty goals to place on education, but how can we ask for less on behalf of our children? Montessori education—*implemented as designed*—may well be a comprehensive intervention to improve the well-being of children from infancy through adolescence and adulthood.

However, there's one caveat: Montessori education is more than the sum of its parts. In other words, it may be possible to add Montessori materials to conventional classrooms or implement instructional approaches used in Montessori classrooms and successfully achieve positive student outcomes. But to realize the true vision of Montessori education—to create a new humanity—we must consider the totality of the Montessori pedagogy: the materials, the educator, the learning environment, along with a deep understanding of the developmental needs of learners across the life span if we are to achieve human flourishing—where harmony and understanding reign and all beings live in peace.

References

1000 Days. (n.d.) *Why 1000 days*. https://thousanddays.org/why-1000-days/

Ahlquist, E.-M. T. (2023). Learning in the Montessori school environment. In A. K. Murray, E.-M. Tebano Ahlquist, M. K. McKenna, & M. Debs (Eds.), *The Bloomsbury handbook of Montessori education* (pp. 117–127). Bloomsbury Academic.

American Montessori Society. (2023). *School accreditation standards*. https://amshq.org/wp-content/uploads/2025/01/2023-AMS-School-Accreditation-Standards.pdf

American Montessori Society. (2025). *Fast facts: Public Montessori schools*. https://amshq.org/about-montessori/press-kit/public-schools/

American Montessori Society. (n.d.-a). *Montessori terminology*. American Montessori Society. https://amshq.org/About-Montessori/What-Is-Montessori/Terminology#:~:text=Sensitive%20period%20%E2%80%93%20A%20critical%20time,the%20development%20of%20that%20skill

American Montessori Society. (n.d.-b). *Montessori secondary programs*. https://amshq.org/About-Montessori/Inside-the-Montessori-Classroom/Secondary

Anderson, J., & Winthrop, R. (January 2, 2025). *Giving kids some autonomy has surprising results*. Guest Essay, New York Times. https://www.nytimes.com/2025/01/02/opinion/children-choices-goal-setting.html

Ansari, A., & Winsler, A. (2020). The long-term benefits of Montessori preK for Latinx children from LOW-INCOME FAMILIES. *Applied Developmental Science, 26*(2), 252–266.

Archer, A., & Hughes, C. A. (2011). *Explicit instruction: Effective and efficient teaching*. Guilford Press.

Asmamaw, M., & Belay, Z. (2021). Mechanism and application of CRISPR/Cas-9-mediated genome editing. *Biologics: Targets and Therapy*, *15*, 353–361. http://doi.org/10.2147/BTT.S326422

Association Montessori Internationale. (n.d.-a). *Montessori educators*. https://montessori-ami.org/about-montessori/montessori-educators

Association Montessori Internationale. (n.d.-b). *Montessori 0–3*. https://montessori-ami.org/about-montessori/montessori-0-3

Association Montessori Internationale. (n.d.-c). *Montessori 3–6*. https://montessori-ami.org/about-montessori/montessori-3-6

Association Montessori Internationale. (n.d.-d). *Montessori elementary (6–12)*. https://montessori-ami.org/about-montessori/montessori-6-12

Association Montessori Internationale. (n.d.-e). *Montessori (12–18)*. https://montessori-ami.org/about-montessori/montessori-12-18

Association Montessori Internationale. (n.d.-f). *Timeline of Maria Montessori's life*. https://montessori-ami.org/resource-library/facts/timeline-maria-montessoris-life

Barron, M. (1983). *Sensorial ideas: Innovative enrichment activities for the Montessori Sensorial area.* Cloice Fannin Graphics.

Blumenthal, H., & Pianta, R. C. (2024). *Kids on earth: The power & potential of 5 billion minds. Pre-publication issue.* www.kidsonearth.org

Borbolla, G. (Winter 2020). Connecting Montessori to the world. *The NAMTA Journal, 4*(14), 89–103.

Bransford, J. D., Brown, A. L., & Cocking, R. R. (2000). *How people learn: Brain, mind, experience, and school.* National Academies Press.

Breiman, R., & Coe, B. (Summer 2016). Why sixth-graders should be in a Montessori upper elementary program. *Montessori Life, 28*(2), 46–49.

Bronfenbrenner, U. (1979.) *The ecology of human development.* Harvard University Press.

Brooks, D. (January 9, 2025). *The character building tool-kit.* The New York Times. https://www.nytimes.com/2025/01/09/opinion/character-building-education.html

Brown, K., Powell, K., & Woodford, L. (2024). *Montessori: Evidence based reading curricula.* Arizona Charter Schools Association and National Center for Montessori in the Public Sector. www.azed.gov/sites/default/files/2024/07/Montessori%20an%20Evidence%20Based%20Reading%20Curricula.pdf

Brunold-Conesa, C. (2025). *Practical life through the ages, part three—Secondary: The adolescent's drive towards social independence.* Montessori Life. American Montessori Society. https://amshq.org/blog/community/practical-life-through-the-ages-part-three-secondary-the-adolescents-drive-toward-social-independence/

California Department of Education. (2008). *The California preschool learning foundations (Volume 1).* Child Development Division, California Department of Education through a contract with WestEd. https://www.cde.ca.gov/sp/cd/re/documents/preschoollf.pdf

CASEL (n.d.). *FAQs: Frequently asked questions about social emotional learning and about CASEL.* https://casel.org/faq

Center for the Developing Child. (n.d.). *What is executive function? And how does it relate to child development?* https://developingchild.harvard.edu/resources/what-is-executive-function-and-how-does-it-relate-to-child-development

Center for the Developing Child. (2017). *5 steps for brain-building serve and return.* https://developingchild.harvard.edu/resources/briefs/5-steps-for-brain-building-serve-and-return

Chen, Y., Cowden, R. G., Fulks, J., Plake, J. F., & VanderWeele, T. J. (2022). National data on age gradients in well-being among U.S. adults. *JAMA psychiatry, 79*(10), 1046–1047.

Coe, B. & Donahoe, M. (n.d.) *Characteristics of an American Montessori Society secondary program.* http://cmstep.com/wp-content/uploads/AMS-Secondary-Position-Paper.pdf

Conesa, C. (2023). *Practical life through the ages, part one—Early childhood: The drive toward physical autonomy.* The Montessori Life blog of the American Montessori Society. https://amshq.org/Blog/2023-10-23-Practical-Life-Through-the-Ages-Part-One-Early-Childhood

Culclasure, B., Fleming, D. J., Riga, G., & Sprogis, A. (2018). *An evaluation of Montessori education in South Carolina's public schools.* The Riley Institute at Furman University. https://www.furman.edu/wp-content/uploads/sites/195/rileypdfFiles/MontessoriOverallResultsFINAL.pdf

Cunningham, J. (2017). From cosmic education to civic responsibility. *The NAMTA Journal, 42*(3), 19–28.

Danielson, C. F. (2009). *Talk about teaching! Leading professional conversations*. Corwin.

Dean, A., LeMoine, S., & Mayoral, A. (2019). *ZERO TO THREE: Critical competencies for infant-toddler educators*. Zero to Three.

Debs, M. C., & Brown, K. E. (2017). Students of color and public Montessori schools: A review of the literature. *Journal of Montessori Research*, *3*(1), 1–15.

Diamond, A. (2015). Research that helps move us closer to a world where each child thrives. *Research in Human Development*, *12*, 288–294. http://doi.org/10.1080/15427609.2015.1068034

Donahoe, M., HildeBrandt Cichucki, P., Coad-Bernard, S., Coe, B., & Scholtz, B. (2013). Best practices in Montessori secondary programs. *Montessori Life*, *25*(2), 16–23.

Dowell, E. (n.d.) *Production and exchange . . . Where'd microeconomy go?* International Montessori Training Institute Blog. https://www.montessori-imti.org/blog/wherediddmicroeconomygo

Duckworth, A. (n.d.-a). *Character lab playbook—Purpose*. https://characterlab.org/playbooks/purpose

Duckworth, A. (n.d.-b). *Character lab playbook—Social intelligence*. https://characterlab.org/playbooks/social-intelligence

Duckworth, A. (n.d.-c). *Character lab playbook—Kindness*. https://characterlab.org/playbooks/kindness

Duckworth, A. (n.d.-d). *Character lab playbook—Curiosity*. https://characterlab.org/playbooks/curiosity

Duckworth, A. (n.d.-e). *Character lab playbook—Grit*. https://characterlab.org/playbooks/grit

Duckworth, A. (n.d.-f). *Character lab playbook—Gratitude*. https://characterlab.org/playbooks/gratitude

Duckworth, A. (n.d.-g). *Character lab playbook—Proactivity*. https://characterlab.org/playbooks/proactivity

Duckworth, A. (n.d.-h). *Character lab playbook—Judgment*. https://characterlab.org/playbooks/judgment

Duckworth, A. (n.d.-i). *Character lab playbook—The Holy Trinity of healthy relationships*. https://characterlab.org/tips-of-the-week/trinity-of-healthy-relationships

Duckwork, A. (n.d.-j). *Small wonders*. https://characterlab.org/tips-of-the-week/small-wonders/

Duckworth, A. (2024). *Heart, mind, will: What character is and why it matters*. https://characterlab.org/tips-of-the-week/heart-mind-will/

Duckworth, A. (2025). *Character lab—about*. https://characterlab.org/about

Duffy, M., & Duffy, D. (2016). *Children of the universe: Cosmic education in the Montessori elementary classroom*. Parent Child Press.

Everett, P. (2024). *James*. Doubleday.

Fierson, P.R. (2023). *The moral philosophy of Maria Montessori: Agency and ethical life*. Bloomsbury Academic.

Fisher, D. & Frey, N. (2021). *Better learning through structured teaching: A framework for the gradual release of responsibility* (3rd ed.). ASCD.

Galinsky, E. (2024). *The breakthrough years: A new scientific framework for raising thriving teens*. Flatiron Books.

Gallahue, D. L., Ozmun, J. C., & Goodway, J. (2012). *Understanding motor development: Infants, children, adolescents, adults*. McGraw-Hill.

Gallup, Inc. (2024). *Walton Family Foundation Gallup Voices of Gen Z Study Year 2 Annual Survey Report.* Walton Foundation. https://nextgeninsights.waltonfamilyfoundation.org/wp-content/uploads/2024/08/Walton_Gallup_Voices-of-Gen-Z_Year-2-2024-Final-Report.pdf

Gallup, Inc. (2025). *The global flourishing study. What contributes to a life well-lived?* Gallup. https://globalflourishingstudy.com/wp-content/uploads/2025/04/GFS_Report-1.pdf

García Coll, C., Lamberty, G., Jenkins, R., McAdoo, H. P., Crnic, K., Wasik, B., & García, H. V. (1996). An integrative model for the study of developmental competencies in minority children. *Child Development*, 67, 1891–1914. https://doi.org/10.2307/1131600

Gettman, D. (1987). *Basic Montessori: Learning activities for under-fives.* St. Martin's Press.

Hainstock, E. G. (1978/1986). *The essential Montessori.* New American Library.

Hayes, N., O'Toole, L., & Halpenny, A. M. (2023). *Introducing Bronfenbrenner: A guide for practitioners and students in early years education* (2nd ed.). Routledge.

Henke, E. (2017). Moral development: From cosmic education to adolescent action. *The NAMTA Journal, 42*(3), 31–41.

Homfray, M., & Child, P. (1983). *Sensorial education.* Montessori World Education Institute.

Honegger, S. (2023). The Montessori approach to children 0–3 years based on Grazia Honegger Fresco's studies. In A. K. Murray, E. M. Tabano Ahlquist, M. K. McKenna, & M. Debs (Eds.). *The Bloomsbury handbook of Montessori education* (pp. 129–136). Bloomsbury Academic.

Horowitz, F. D., Darling-Hammond, L., & Bransford, J., with Comer, J., Rosebrock, K., Austin, K., & Rust, F. (2005). Educating teachers for developmentally appropriate practice. In L. Darling-Hammond & J. Bransford (Eds.), *Preparing teachers for a changing world: What teachers should learn and be able to do* (pp. 88–125). Jossey-Bass.

Huneke-Stone, E. (2015). *Grace and courtesy in the elementary classroom.* Presentation at NAMTA conference titled Grace, Courtesy, and Civility Across the Planes, Portland, OR, March 13–16, 2024.

Hutchinson, D. (Winter 2013). Teaching nature: From philosophy to practice. *The NAMTA Journal, 38*(1), 195. https://files.eric.ed.gov/fulltext/EJ1077989.pdf

Indrio,. F., Pietrobelli, A., Dargenio, V. N., Marchese, F., Grillo, A., Vural, M., Giardino, I., & Pettoello-Mantovani, M. (2023). The key 1000 life-changing days. *Global Pediatrics*, 4, 100049. https://www.sciencedirect.com/science/article/pii/S2667009723000155

International Montessori Council. (2024). *School accreditation handbook.* https://drive.google.com/file/d/13Et1uN3UuOV5Kyf3aTHYGKSDIUMFFEEt/view

Kessler, R. (2000). *The soul of education: Helping students find connection, compassion, and character at school.* Association for Supervision and Curriculum Development.

Kuhl, P. (2010). *The linguistic genius of babies.* TED Talk. https://www.ted.com/talks/patricia_kuhl_the_linguistic_genius_of_babies

Lally, J. R. (2009). *The science and psychology of infant–toddler care: How an understanding of early learning has transformed child care.* Zero to Three.

Lansbury, A. (2013). *Bonding with babies: Where RIE and attachment parenting differ.* https://www.janetlansbury.com/2013/03/bonding-with-babies-where-rie-and-attachment-parenting-differ/

Leonard, G. (Spring 2015). The Montessori classroom: A foundation for global citizenship. *The NAMTA Journal,* 40(2), 91–110.

Leonard, G. (Summer 2018). Maria Montessori's cosmic stories and contemporary science. *The NAMTA Journal, 43*(3), *33–45.*

Leonard, G., & Allen, K. (Spring 2021). Experiences in nature: Resolute second-plane directions toward Erdkinder. *The NAMTA Journal, 45*(1), 81–98.

Levin, D. E. (2013). *Beyond remote-controlled childhood: Teaching young children in the media age.* National Association for the Education of Young Children.

Lillard, A. S., Meyer, M. J., Vasc, D., & Fukuda, E. (2021). An association between Montessori education in childhood and adult wellbeing. *Frontiers in Psychology,* 12, 721943. http://doi.org/10.3389/fpsyg.2021.721943

Lnenickovä, I. (2015). *Montessori language teaching: Materials analysis and evaluation.* Master's thesis, Masaryk University.

Ludick, P. (Winter 2014). The positive personality of the Montessori adolescent. *The NAMTA Journal, 39*(1), 142–159.

Ludick, P., Reyers, J., Waski, M., Kjaer, C., Schaefer, L., Moudry, J., & Davis, L. (2009). The new adolescent ages 12–15 and 15–18: Optimal roadmaps for discipline-based studies. *The NAMTA Journal, 34*(3), 267–274.

Maier, W. (2023). The Montessori elementary school for children ages 6–12. In A. K. Murray, E.-M. Tebano Ahlquist, M. K. McKenna, & M. Debs (Eds.), *The Bloomsbury handbook of Montessori education* (pp. 147–155). Bloomsbury Academic.

Mallett, J. D., & Schroeder, J. L. (2015). Academic achievement outcomes: A comparison of Montessori and non-Montessori public elementary school students. *Journal of Elementary Education, 25*(1), 39–53.

McDevitt, T. M., & Ormrod, J. E. (2013). *Child development and education* (5th ed.). Pearson.

Millie, Terry (2026). Hexavium—*A visual representation of the Montessori 6–12 curriculum.* https://qrco.de/bfjaQe

Montessori Public Policy Institute. (2015). *Montessori essentials.* https://montessoriadvocacy.org/wp-content/uploads/2019/07/MontessoriEssentials.pdf

Montessori, M. (1946). *The 1946 London Lectures, Lecture 22 "Movement and Character."* Montessori-Pierson Publishing Company.

Montessori, M. (1948). *Discovery of the child.* Associated Printers. https://ia601505.us.archive.org/32/items/in.ernet.dli.2015.110354/2015.110354.The-Discovery-Of-The-Child.pdf

Montessori, M. (1948/1955). *To educate the human potential.* Kalakshetra Publications. https://archive.org/stream/in.ernet.dli.2015.136487/2015.136487.To-Educate-The-Human-Potential-Ed-2nd_djvu.txt

Montessori, M. (1948/2007). *From childhood to adolescence.* Montessori Pierson Publishing. https://ia803003.us.archive.org/14/items/fromchildhoodtoadolescentmariamontessoripdfdrive.com1/From%20Childhood%20to%20Adolescent%20-%20Maria%20Montessori%20%28%20PDFDrive.com%20%29%20%281%29_text.pdf

Montessori, M. (1949). Educazione e Pace. Opera Montessori. In A. K. Murray, E. -M. Tebano Ahlquist, M. K. McKenna, & M. Debs (Eds.), *The Bloomsbury handbook of Montessori education* (pp. 29–35). Bloomsbury Academic.

Montessori, M. (1949/1964). *Education and peace.* Translation of Maria Montessori's original article, Peace and Education, by Cristina Gaggioli, Giorgia Montanucci, Loredana Fabbri. Article provided as part of Maria Montessori: Pedagogy and Peace, a course offered by University for Foreigners of Perugia, Italy. https://www.unistrapg.it/en/studying-at-unistrapg/advanced-training/advanced-training-course-maria-montessori-pedagogy-for-peace

Montessori, M. (1955/1989). *The formation of man.* Clio Press.

Montessori, M. (1967/1995). *The absorbent mind.* Henry Holt & Co.

Montessori, M. (2007). *Maria Montessori speaks to parents: A selection of articles, Volume 21 of Montessori series.* Montessori-Pierson Publishing. https://montessori-pierson.com/products/maria-montessori-speaks-to-parents-vol-21

Montessori Jr., Mario M. (1976). *Education for human development: Understanding Montessori.* Schocken Books.

Moore, T. G., Arefadib, N., Deery, A., & West, S. (2017). *The first thousand days: An evidence paper.* Parkville, Victoria, Centre for Community Child Health, Murdoch Children's Research Institute.

Moretti, E. (2022). *The best weapon for peace: Maria Montessori, education, and children's rights.* University of Wisconsin Press.

Morgan, H. J., & Saylor, L. (2024). Research and observation: Pedagogical essentials for building a better world. In *Montessori in contemporary culture* (p. 17–34). American Montessori Society.

Murthy, V. (2025). *As he concludes his second tenure, 21st U.S. Surgeon General issues parting prescription for America.* U.S. Department of Health and Human Services. https://www.hhs.gov/about/news/2025/01/07/21st-surgeon-general-issues-parting-prescription-for-america.html

Myers, K. (2017). Designing Montessori discipline frameworks for all settings. *The NAMTA Journal, 42*(3), 43–47.

National Academies of Sciences, Engineering, and Medicine. (2015). *Transforming the workforce for children birth through age 8: A unifying foundation.* The National Academies Press. https://doi.org/10.17226/19401

National Academies of Sciences, Engineering, and Medicine. (2024). *A new vision for high-quality preschool curriculum.* The National Academies Press. https://doi.org/10.17226/27429

National Academies of Sciences, Engineering, and Medicine; Health and Medicine Division; Division of Behavioral and Social Sciences and Education; Board on Children, Youth, and Families; Committee on the Neurobiological and Socio-behavioral Science of Adolescent Development and Its Applications; Backes, E. P, & Bonnie, R. J. (Eds.). (2019). *The promise of adolescence: Realizing opportunity for all youth.* National Academies Press. https://www.ncbi.nlm.nih.gov/books/NBK545476

National Association for the Education of Young Children. (2022). *Developmentally Appropriate Practice in Early Childhood Programs* (4th ed.). NAEYC.

National Association for the Education of Young Children. (2020). *NAEYC position statement: Developmentally appropriate practice.* NAEYC.

National Research Council & Institute of Medicine. (2000). *From neurons to neighborhoods: The science of early childhood development.* J. P. Shonkoff & D. A. Phillips, Eds., Board of Children, Youth, and Families, Commission on Behavioral and Social Sciences and Education. National Academy Press.

National Scientific Council on the Developing Child. (2023). *Place matters: The environment we create shapes the foundations of healthy development* (Working Paper No. 16). Harvard University. https://developingchild.harvard.edu

National Scientific Council on the Developing Child. (2007). *In brief: The science of early childhood development.* Harvard University. https://developingchild.harvard.edu/resources/inbriefs/inbrief-science-of-ecd/

National Scientific Council on the Developing Child. (2020). *Connecting the brain to the rest of the body: Early childhood development and lifelong health are deeply intertwined* (Working Paper No. 15). Harvard University. https://developingchild.harvard.edu/wp-content/uploads/2024/10/wp15_health_FINALv2.pdf

Nelson, D. (2023). *Pedagogical approaches and the role of equity maps.* Doctoral dissertation, Wilkes University.

O'Shaughnessy, M. (Summer 2016a). The observation scientist. *The NAMTA Journal, 41*(3), 57–99.

O'Shaughnessy, M. (Summer 2016b). The observation artist. *The NAMTA Journal, 41*(3), 1–39.

Orem, R. C. (1974). *Montessori: Her method and movement—What you need to know.* Putnam.

Orion, J. (2009). Normalization under three. *The NAMTA Journal, 34*(1), 79–89.

Orr, D. W. (2018). The (missing) politics in environmental and sustainability education. *The NAMTA Journal, 41*(3), 36–50.

Palmer, P. J. (1998). Evoking the spirit in public education. *Educational Leadership, 56*(4). https://www.ascd.org/el/articles/evoking-the-spirit-in-public-education

Park, D., Tsukayama, E., Goodwin, G. P., Patrick, S., & Duckworth, A. (2017). A tripartite taxonomy of character: Evidence for intrapersonal, interpersonal, and intellectual competencies in children. *Contemporary Educational Psychology, 48*, 16–27.

Paul, A. M. (2021). *The extended mind: The power of thinking outside the brain.* Houghton Mifflin Harcourt.

Perry, A. (2024). Upholding our history: Tracing Montessori from past to present. In H. Gerker & C. Jones (Eds.), *Montessori in contemporary culture* (pp. 7–15). American Montessori Society.

Philipart, H. (n.d.). *Montessori Guide—An introduction to practical life.* Association Montessori Internationale. https://montessoriguide.org/an-introduction-to-practical-life

Quattrocchi Montanaro, S. (1991). *Understanding the human being: The importance of the first three years of life.* Nienhuis Montessori USA.

Quattrocchi Montanaro, S. (Winter 2009). Why it is important to know the child. *The NAMTA Journal, 34*(1), 2–7. https://archives.montessori-ami.org/do/6de96148-64bc-4dfc-a39c-30d55cd8a960

Raimondo, R. (2023). Cosmic Education: The vital center of the Montessori perspective. In A. K. Murray, E.-M. Tebano Ahlquist, M. K. McKenna, & M. Debs (Eds.), *The Bloomsbury handbook of Montessori education* (pp. 29–35). Bloomsbury Academic.

Ramani, U. (Spring 2013). Practical life: The keystone of life, culture, and community. *The NAMTA Journal, 38*(2), 47–54. https://archives.montessori-ami.org/do/50af85f3-4e99-4b99-b566-1030e2dd7537#mode/2up

Ramani, U. (2023). The Children's House for children ages 3–6. In A. K. Murray, E.-M. Tebano Ahlquist, M. K. McKenna, & M. Debs (Eds.), *The Bloomsbury handbook of Montessori education* (pp.137–145). Bloomsbury Academic.

Rambusch, N. M. (1962/2012). *Learning how to learn: An American approach to Montessori* (Commemorative Edition). Parent Child Press and the American Montessori Society.

Sackett, G. (2015). Grace and courtesy: Empowering children, liberating adults. *The NAMTA Journal, 40*(1), 113–126.

Sackett, G. (Spring 2016). The scientist in the classroom: The Montessori teacher as scientist. *The NAMTA Journal, 41*(2), 5–20.

Scocchera, A. (Ed). (2002). *Il metodo del bambino e la formazione dell'uomo. Scritti e documenti inediti e rari.* Edizioni Opera Nazionale Montessori, Rome, p. 197.

Seldin, T. (2023). *Discover, grow, valorize: Montessori's journey for adolescents.* Montessori Foundation. https://www.montessori.org/discover-grow-valorize-montessoris-journey-for-adolescents/#:~:text=The%20Montessori%20term%20valorization%20of,Montessori%20offers%20a%20refreshing%20departure.

Seldin, T., & Raymond, D. (1981). *Geography and history for the young child.* Brigham Young University Press.

Shelton, L. G. (2019). *The Bronfenbrenner primer: A guide to develecology.* Routledge.

Shivji, M., & Taliaferro Lofquist, G. (2024). Paving the path to a transformative future. In H. Gerker & C. Jones (Eds.), *Montessori in contemporary culture* (pp. 185–203). American Montessori Society.

Sizer, T. R. (1985). *Horace's compromise: The dilemma of the American high school.* Houghton Mifflin.

Snyder, A. L., Tong, X., & Lillard, A. S. (2022). Standardized test proficiency in public Montessori schools. *Journal of School Choice, 16*(1), 105–135.

Stambler, A. (2013). *14. Civic literacy. Literacies for the digital age to teach in the K-12 classroom.* Pier Institute, Global Youth in the Digital Age, Yale University. https://pier.macmillan.yale.edu/sites/default/files/files/Global%20Youth%20in%20the%20Digital%20Age/14_%20CIVIC%20LITERACY.pdf

Stephenson, S. M. (2012). *The red corolla: Montessori cosmic education introduction for ages 3–6+.* Michael Olaf Montessori Publishing.

Suhor, C. (1998). Spirituality—Letting it grow in the classroom. *Educational Leadership.* https://www.ascd.org/el/articles/spirituality-letting-it-grow-in-the-classroom

Teachstone. (2023). *Reference manual: Classroom Assessment Scoring System, PreK-3rd grade* (2nd ed.). Teachstone, Inc.

Trabalzini, P. (Spring 2011). Maria Montessori through the seasons: The "Method." *The NAMTA Journal, 36*(2), Xi.

UNICEF & Gallup. (2021). *The changing childhood project: A multigenerational, international survey on 21st century childhood.* https://www.unicef.org/innocenti/media/566/file/UNICEF-Global-Insight-Gallup-Changing-Childhood-Survey-Report-English-2021.pdf

Van der Weel, F. R., & Van der Meer, A. L. H. (2024). Handwriting but not typewriting leads to widespread brain connectivity: A high-density EEG study with implications for the classroom. *Frontiers in Psychology, 14.* https://doi.org/10.3389/fpsyg.2023.1219945

VanderWeele, T. (2024). *The Global Flourishing Study: Study profile and initial results on flourishing.* Research Square. https://doi.org/10.21203/rs.3.rs-5312412/v1

Waski, M. (2017). How the mathematical mind of the adolescent develops from early adolescence to later adolescence. *The NAMTA Journal,* 42(3), 5–16.

World Economic Forum. (2025). *Future of jobs report.* https://reports.weforum.org/docs/WEF_Future_of_Jobs_Report_2025.pdf

ZERO TO THREE. (n.d.). *Why 0–3.* https://www.zerotothree.org/why-0-3/

ZERO TO THREE. (2023). *Infant and early childhood mental health guiding principles.* Zero to Three.

Zoll, S., Ansari, A., & Saylor, L. (2023). Assessment in Montessori education. In A. K. Murray, E.-M. Tebano Ahlquist, M. K. McKenna, & M. Debs (Eds.), *The Bloomsbury handbook of Montessori education* (pp. 219–229). Bloomsbury Academic.

Zoll, S., Feinberg, N., & Saylor, L. (2023). *Powerful literacy in the Montessori classroom: Aligning reading research and practice.* Teachers College Press.

Montessori Constellation

This document lists a fraction of the many organizations and initiatives that support Montessori educators and school administrators across all, presented in alphabetical order.

American Montessori Society (AMS): https://amshq.org/
- AMS Archive at University of Connecticut: https://lib.uconn.edu/location/asc/collections/amsrecords
- AMS Research Library: https://amshq.org/research-library/
- AMS Journal of Montessori Research (in collaboration with University of Kansas): https://journals.ku.edu/jmr
- Regional Action Commission: https://amshq.org/about-montessori/regional-action-commission
- Resources for Montessori Research: https://amshq.org/resources-for-research
- Publications: https://amshq.org/educators/community/special-publications

Association Montessori Internationale (AMI)
- AMI-USA: https://amiusa.org
- AMI Research: https://montessori-ami.org/resource-library/research
- AMI Resource Library: https://montessori-ami.org/resource-library

Center for Montessori Studies—Hartford University: www.hartford.edu/academics/schools-colleges/enhp/research/center-for-montessori-studies.aspx#accordion-group-2-section-2-label

Cincinnati Montessori Secondary Teacher Education (CMStep): https://cmstep.com

Loyola University: www.loyola.edu/school-education/academics/graduate/montessori

Maitri Learning: https://www.maitrilearning.com

Montessori Accreditation Council for Teacher Education (MACTE): www.macte.org
- MontessoriPublic: www.montessoripublic.org
- Montessori Census: https://montessoricensus.org
- TeachMontessori: https://teach-montessori.org

Montessori for Aging and Dementia: https://brushdevelopment.com/montessori-for-aging-and-dementia

Montessori for Dementia, Disability, and Ageing: https://mdda.montessori-ami.org
Montessori Educational Programs International (MEPI): www.mepiinc.com
Montessori and Elder Care/Dementia: https://amshq.org/blog/dementia/the-montessori-method-applied-to-dementia (article)
Montessori Foundation: www.montessori.org
Montessori Institute—New England: https://mi-ne.org
Montessori Medical Partnerships for Inclusion: https://montessori4inclusion.org
Montessori-Pierson Publishing: https://montessori-pierson.com
Montessori Public Policy Initiative (MPPI): https://montessoriadvocacy.org
List of state advocacy groups: https://montessoriadvocacy.org/connect/find-a-state-group
What We Know About What We Do: https://montessoriadvocacy.org/white-papers
Montessori Research Collective: https://montessoriresearchcollective.org/current-mrc-partners
Montessori Science Program—University of Virginia: https://communitypartnerships.virginia.edu/montessori-science-program
Montessori Services: www.montessoriservices.com
Montessori Sports: www.montessori-sports.com
Montessori Teacher Education Institute of Atlanta https://www.montessoriteachered.com/
Montessori Training Center Northeast (MTCNE): www.mtcne.org
Montessori on Wheels: www.montessorionwheels.org
National Center for Montessori in the Public Sector (NCMPS): www.public-montessori.org
Nienhuis (Montessori materials): www.nienhuis.com/us
North American Montessori Teacher Association (NAMTA): https://montessori-namta.org
Sarasota University: www.sarasotauniversity.edu
Seton Montessori Institute: https://www.setonmontessori.org/smi-home
Shelton Montessori Training (includes inclusion): www.shelton.org/shelton-teacher-training/montessori
University of Wisconsin—River Falls: www.uwrf.edu/Montessori-EdD
Utah Montessori Council: https://utahmontessori.org
Virginia Montessori Association (VMA): www.virginiamontessoriassociation.org
Xavier University: www.xavier.edu/montessori/index

MONTESSORI INFLUENCERS

Authors

Joseph Campbell (publisher): https://learningsunshine.org/shopping

Simone Davies and Junnifa Uzodike (2024). *The Montessori Child.* Workman Publishing.

Mira Debs (2021). *Diverse Families, Desirable Schools: Public Montessori in the Era of School Choice.* Harvard Education Press.

Jana Morgan Herman (2025). *Materials Manual 1946 India Lectures Course. Book One Practical Life.* Self published.

Angeline Lillard (2017). *The Science Behind the Genius.* Oxford University Press.

Catherine McTamaney (2007). *The Tao of Montessori: Reflections on Compassionate Teaching.* IUniverse.

Erica Moretti (2021). *The Best Weapon for Peace: Maria Montessori, Education, and Children's Rights.* University of Wisconsin Press.

Joyce Pickering & Sylvia O. Richardson (2019). *Montessori Strategies for Children With Learning Differences: The MACAR Model.* Parent Child Press.

Paula Lillard Preschlack (2023). *The Montessori Potential.* Chicago Review Press.

Susan Mayclin Stephenson (2013). *The Joyful Child: Montessori, Global Wisdom for Birth to Three.* Michael Olaf Montessori Company.

Katie Keller Woods (2025). *Alignment: A Montessori Approach to Reimagining Work-Life Balance.* Page Two.

Work With Families

Pamela Green—Ananda Montessori: www.instagram.com/ananda montessori/?hl=en

Zil Jager—literacy: www.instagram.com/ziljaeger/?hl=en

Lucie Tamášová—Montessori Parenting: www.montessoriparenting.org/

Podcasts/Blogs

American Montessori Society—Educating the Human Potential: https://amshq.org/podcast

Association Montessori Internationale: https://podcasts.apple.com/us/podcast/ami-podcasts/id1468955744

Jess Davis: https://podcasts.apple.com/us/podcast/roots-and-wings-montessori-podcast/id1767936862

Andrew Faulstich: https://breakingtheparadigm.org

Margaret Jarrell: https://greenspringcenter.org/podcast
Elizabeth Slade: https://montessori-action.org/podcast-index
Margaret Whitley: https://margaretwhitley.substack.com
Susan Zoll: https://montessorilogospraxis.substack.com

Index

About the Authors

Trisha Thompson-Willingham began her Montessori journey in 1992. Thirty-three years later, she has the perspective of a parent, guide, coach, administrator, and independent school board member. She has worked as a reading specialist and a special educator. Trisha holds a Master of Education with a specialty in Montessori Elementary and is trained in Montessori at three levels: 0–3, 3–6, and 6–12, as well as an orientation to adolescence. She co-founded and led the Virginia Montessori Association for 8 years and served on the Montessori Public Policy Initiative's Board of Directors, whose mission is to increase access to Montessori Education in the United States.

Susan Zoll holds a PhD in Education and a Montessori Early Childhood (3–6) credential, having served as a Montessori educator, teacher trainer, Head of School, board member, and tenured associate professor. Her research speaks to the need for increased access to learner-centered classrooms that support all children's development. She has served in leadership roles on several projects funded by the U.S. Department of Education, working alongside school administrators, educators, and families to support student learning. Susan served on the American Montessori Society's Research Committee and was awarded the AMS Impact Award. She is a frequent speaker at national conferences and has co-authored two additional books published by Teachers College Press: *Powerful Literacy in the Montessori Classroom: Aligning Reading Research and Practice* (2023) and *Effective Literacy Assessment in the Montessori Classroom: Using Data to Inform Instruction* (2025). To learn more about her work visit: www.dr-susan-zoll.com.